Lifelines

CREATING MEMORY ART
TO CHRONICLE YOUR
personal connections

CAROL WINGERT
& TENA SPRENGER

NORTH LIGHT BOOKS
Cincinnati, Ohio

www.artistsnetwork.com

11 10 09 08 07   5 4 3 2 1

Library of Congress Cataloging-in-Publication Data

Wingert, Carol.
  Lifelines : creating memory art to chronicle your personal connections / by Carol Wingert and Tena Sprenger.
      p. cm.
  Includes index.
  ISBN-13: 978-1-58180-886-5 (pbk. : alk. paper)
  ISBN-10: 1-58180-886-0 (pbk. : alk. paper)
  1. Photograph albums. 2. Photographs--Conservation and restoration. 3. Scrapbooks. I. Sprenger, Tena.
  II. Title.
  TR501.W565 2007
  745.593--dc22
                            2006028007

Distributed in Canada by Fraser Direct
100 Armstrong Avenue
Georgetown, ON, Canada L7G 5S4
Tel: (905) 877-4411

Distributed in the U.K. and Europe by David & Charles
Brunel House, Newton Abbot, Devon, TQ12 4PU, England
Tel: (+44) 1626 323200, Fax: (+44) 1626 323319
E-mail: postmaster@davidandcharles.co.uk

Distributed in Australia by Capricorn Link
P.O. Box 704, South Windsor, NSW 2756 Australia
Tel: (02) 4577-3555

EDITORS: JESSICA GORDON AND JESSICA STRAWSER
DESIGNER: MARISSA BOWERS
LAYOUT ARTIST: CHERYL MATHAUER
PRODUCTION COORDINATOR: GREG NOCK
PHOTOGRAPHERS: CHRISTINE POLOMSKY AND TIM GRONDIN
PHOTO STYLIST: JAN NICKUM

fw
F+W PUBLICATIONS, INC.

Acknowledgments

We would like to say thanks to our editors, Jessica Gordon and Jessica Strawser, and to Marissa Bowers and Christine Polomsky at F+W Publications, for your guidance and support, and your professionalism and warmth. You have all made this project a delight for us. And, to Christine Doyle, a special thanks for another opportunity to share our artistic vision. Thank you also to our layout artist, Cheryl Mathauer, and to our production coordinator, Greg Nock. A special thanks to Kimberly Kwan for doing our bio photos and continuing to make us look good!

Thank you also to our contributing guest artists for your creativity and willingness to share your passion and tell your stories. Finally, we would like to thank you, our readers, for allowing us to share our lifelines and stories with you. In doing so, we hope that you feel more connected with us.

METRIC CONVERSION CHART

TO CONVERT	TO	MULTIPLY BY
Inches	Centimeters	2.54
Centimeters	Inches	0.4
Feet	Centimeters	30.5
Centimeters	Feet	0.03
Yards	Meters	0.9
Meters	Yards	1.1
Sq. Inches	Sq. Centimeters	6.45
Sq. Centimeters	Sq. Inches	0.16
Sq. Feet	Sq. Meters	0.09
Sq. Meters	Sq. Feet	10.8
Sq. Yards	Sq. Meters	0.8
Sq. Meters	Sq. Yards	1.2
Pounds	Kilograms	0.45
Kilograms	Pounds	2.2
Ounces	Grams	28.3
Grams	Ounces	0.035

Dedication

This book is dedicated to Vern and Ashley for their infinite patience and uncomplaining spirit, even when the projects took over most of the house and most of my time; to Mom and Dad for encouraging my creative pursuits and providing many opportunities to learn and grow; and to Mrs. Glorianna Luley, my junior high English teacher, for instilling in me a love and passion for writing. — Carol

I would like to dedicate this book to my parents, Darlene and Ray Pasternak. Throughout my life as well as the book writing process, they have always been there to support me no matter what my request may be, from, "Dad, will a band saw cut through this metal?" to, "Mom, could you possibly find one of these wooden thingies at an auction?" to, "Are you sure you don't mind playing taxi driver to my kids while I am out of town?" I love you both. Thanks is not enough. — Tena

About the Authors

TENA SPRENGER

Tena Sprenger has always loved creative arts and teaching, and combining the two has created her dream job. Tena enjoys teaching at her local scrapbooks store, Scrapbooks, Etc., as well as throughout the United States and internationally as a featured instructor for events such as Creative Escape, Scrap Gala and Day to Create. Tena's artwork is regularly featured in *Creating Keepsakes* magazine, and she was inducted into the Creating Keepsakes Hall of Fame in 2004. Co-author of *Artful Memories*, also from North Light Books, Tena is also a contributing artist for several Autumn Leaves books: *The Book Book*, *Designing with Fabric*, *Designing with Stamps* and *Designing with Paper*. Tena lives in Mesa, Arizona, with her husband, Mike, and her children, Alyssa and Michael. When she is not busy making a creative mess in her art room, she enjoys reading and dance.

CAROL WINGERT

From the time she was a child, Carol Wingert has wanted to teach, create and write. In memory arts, she has found all three passions. Her international teaching experiences include acting as a keynote guest "tutor" at a 2004 scrapbook convention in Australia and serving as an instructor at the 2006 Scrap Gala in New Brunswick, Canada. She has taught at Creating Keepsakes University and Creative Escape. Carol conducts Day to Create classes with Tena across the country, and she also teaches at her local scrapbook stores Ink It! Inc. and Scrapbooks, Etc. Carol is co-author of *Artful Memories*, also by North Light Books. Her work may also be found in six Autumn Leaves "Designing With" books, as well as *The Book Book*, in which she was the lead artist. Carol's art appears in a number of Design Originals publications, and she is a frequent contributor to *Legacy* magazine, where she serves on the Editorial Advisory Board. Carol lives in Gilbert, Arizona, with her husband, Vern, daughter, Ashley, and their menagerie of animals. Her favorite pastimes include gardening, reading, cooking and traveling.

Contents

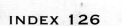

the trials of puppy-hood

MODEL BOY

G GUNDAM ZERO

THIS TODAY

ne Door to
ife is
Wide Open
ry to
so Tight
beGiN to

ven when there are
the instructions are

Introduction

When you see the word *lifeline*, what do you think of? In our dramatic imaginations, we conjure images of someone out in deep water needing to be rescued and someone on shore throwing out a safety rope. But what a lifeline really represents is something that connects those two people.

Memory art—from scrapbook pages to other creative crafts that showcase photos and memorabilia—is all about chronicling the connections, or lifelines, we have in this life with the people, places and things we love. Our lifelines form a legacy that is unique to each of us. When we sat down to create this book, we started thinking about our own lifelines—special relationships, things we cherish, daily routines and other aspects of our histories and our selves that make us strong.

Our minds were buzzing with all the memory art possibilities. Tena was particularly excited about creating art to celebrate the people who were part of making us who we are. She had access to trunks full of memorabilia from her family's past, but had always been too busy documenting family vacations, dance recitals and holidays to tell the old family stories. Tena compiled a list of projects she could create using family heritage photos. The resulting artwork helped her to connect with her past and prompted us to explore other unique ways to use heritage photos in art.

Carol's approach was a bit different. Her collection of memory art was missing something else: anything about her. Her projects always focused on family, friends, travel and nature. Creating this book gave her permission to share her creative side, things she values most, pages of her art journal and her most meaningful relationships. She became excited about personal journaling and even started a blog. We both learned that one of the best things about sharing pieces of ourselves is that others then do the same—and new relationships are born!

So, we combined approaches and divided this book into three sections, all designed to inspire you to create memory art about your own lifelines. The first, "Here and Now," focuses on the people who mean the most to us, how our lives are intertwined, and dreams and goals we share. The second, "Forever Remembered," shares the stories of people, past and present, who have strong influences in our lives. The third, "Express Yourself," explores the aspects of ourselves that we all want to record for future generations.

For each project, we begin by sharing the inspiration behind the art to get your own creative wheels turning. We then offer step-by-step instruction for one key artistic technique that we used in the project and that you could creatively apply or adapt to your own memory art. Along the way you'll find tips on chronicling your own lifelines as well as on constructing your own projects.

We found wisdom in an Arabic proverb: "Every day of your life is a page of your history." We hope this book inspires you to create memory art focusing on your lifelines and using some of the fun and innovative techniques we spotlight here. Focus on everyday relationships, on people who have greatly influenced you, and on yourself—just as we have through sharing our own stories in these pages. We hope that in doing so we form a new lifeline with you.

Supplies

Here's a brief rundown of some things you'll want to have on hand to create your own memory art.

Paper

Certain papers are more suited for specific uses in our projects than others. Here are some of our favorites:

Image Transfer Material (ITM) is a fantastic product we use to transfer images to project surfaces. It is available in 8.5" × 11" (22cm × 28cm) matte-finish adhesive sheets and can be used to make oversized packing tape transfers or clear stickers and text blocks.

Cardstock is available in a variety of sizes, weights, textures and colors. It accepts paint and ink without warping and adds support to embellished scrapbook pages. Unless otherwise noted, we use Bazzill cardstock.

Chipboard is a thin, unfinished cardboard. Use it to make lightweight covers, to create embellishments without adding bulk and to add support to scrapbook pages.

Altering Supplies

In addition to the basics—acrylic paint and brushes—here's what you'll need.

Gesso is a paint-like substance made from ground acrylic that prepares surfaces such as canvas or wood for painting. It is available in white, black and occasionally dark brown. White gesso may also be combined with acrylic paints to lighten them.

Castaway ink, together with the use of a hot, dry iron, changes the color of uncoated paper to give it an almost batik look. This product comes in the form of an ink pad, and it may be used with rubber stamps, on stipple rushes or applied directly to the paper from the pad.

Modeling paste is a lightweight, fast-drying medium made for crafters to create a textured appearance on surfaces such as chipboard, bookboard and wood. Application to the surface may be done with a palette knife or spatula. It may be painted or glazed and also may be stamped into when almost completely dry.

Watercolor crayons can be used dry or blended with a wet brush to create a watercolor motif. Their colors are highly opaque and can be intensified by layering. They work best when applied to watercolor artist paper.

Transfer Mediums

For some of our projects, we transfer images from photos onto other surfaces, including fabric and tile. It's easier than it sounds: All you need is some transfer medium.

Regular gel medium (matte) is an acrylic polymer that is effective in transferring toner or ink-jet copies onto fabric. It's also a great dimensional adhesive, as well as a glazing compound to brush over completed artwork.

Colorless blender markers, or xylene markers, are solvent-based markers used to transfer ink from a toner copy to a receiving paper.

Adhesives

Here are our favorite tried-and-true adhesives.

UHU glue sticks have a trademark pinkish-purple color that turns clear when dry. Colored glue is helpful when gluing paper on a book cover because it makes consistent application easy. We recommend using a brayer when adhering papers with UHU.

PVA glue is archival-quality, acid-free white glue that is popular with book artists and is effective for gluing down handmade papers, which can be quite thick.

Mod Podge is a découpage medium used as an adhesive as well as a finish or protective coat over paper.

Diamond Glaze is a dimensional adhesive that is used to adhere embellishments or is brushed over the artwork for a clear, high-gloss, glass-like finish.

Tacky Glue and **Thick Designer Tacky Glue** are multipurpose, fairly inexpensive white glue products used to adhere embellishments. They dry clear.

E-6000 glue is an exceptional dimensional adhesive that may be used on wood, metal and glass. Drying time can be longer than other adhesives, but the bond is permanent.

Perfect Paper Adhesive (PPA) is similar to PVA and is available in both gloss and matte finish. It works well as a protective coating on paper, especially in matte finish.

Smoothing, Folding and Piercing Tools

These are the must-have tools to get started.

A **brayer** is a handheld rolling tool that smooths air bubbles and wrinkles on adhered paper surfaces. Brayers often come with interchangeable rollers.

A **bone folder** is a handheld tool, with a rounded end and a pointed end, used to score cardstock for folding or to burnish a fold line for a sharp crease.

An **awl** is a handheld tool with a sharp point used primarily by book artists to pierce holes for stitching.

Here and Now

As people, we seem to have a strong need to belong—to belong to a family, to be part of a friendship, to be a member of a club, church or other organization. Living in an age of technology—where interaction with others is often through voice mails, e-mails and Webcams—the connection to other human beings is what grounds us and makes life meaningful. This section focuses on people who mean much to us, how our lives are intertwined, and how these connections contribute to the color of our memories and the quality of our lives.

Carol's most meaningful long-term relationship is with her husband, Vern. After being married to him for more than twenty-nine years, she wanted him to know that he was "Still the One" and created a book for him based on the song lyrics. She loved using pictures of him that expressed different emotions and moods—laughter, reflection, joy, strength and pure happiness.

We all like to see ourselves (at least, our strong points!) in our children. Tena's project titled *Michael's Art* is special to her for that reason. Her son has never been interested in scrapbooking or memory art, but he's always loved writing and illustrating. When Tena suggested they join efforts to create this piece of wall art for the book, he was thrilled. Bubbleman was the first comic book character Michael created, and having this commemorated in a piece of wall art is meaningful to the whole family. Their project reinforced the bond between Michael and Tena in their love of art and their need to express themselves in their own creative ways.

When you sit down and think about all the people you touch in the course of your daily routine, you'll realize that the web of personal connections you weave is truly amazing. These simple and plentiful daily lifelines are the pulse we all check ourselves against when evaluating our progress in life's journey. We hope you use the following ideas to commemorate them in your memory art projects.

COUSIN CONNECTION

by Tena

Connected. Connected by family, memories, love tears, water fights, birthday parties, hugs, Christmas, sleepovers, secrets, connections that will last forever. I hope the friendship and kinship formed in childhood with your cousins keeps you close as you grow up and finds you gathering your families together as we do to continue making connections to last a lifetime.

I was lucky to grow up in a family with an abundance of cousins at my disposal to play with regularly. We got together often on weekends to spend extended periods of time with each other in the summer. Those childhood friendships have turned into some of my closest adult relationships, and my own children are now continuing the tradition. They are very close to their cousins, and I see them **forging friendships that will last a lifetime**.

№ 1

Print a photo on high-gloss photo paper

Copy and paste a high-contrast photo into a Word document, then convert it to a negative image. Print the photo on high-gloss photo paper.

№ 2

Apply alcohol ink

Dip a foam makeup sponge into a puddle of alcohol ink and apply it in light strokes to the photo until the desired color intensity is reached.

№ 3

Punch out photo circles

Use a circular paper punch to cut the photocopied and inked images into regular circles.

№ 4

Adhere circular photos to chipboard

Use monoadhesive to adhere each circular photo to a chipboard circle. Brayer over each circle to secure the image.

SUPPLIES
for the Technique

DIGITAL IMAGE

MICROSOFT WORD

PRINTER

HIGH-GLOSS PHOTO PAPER

FOAM MAKEUP SPONGES

ALCOHOL INKS *(Ranger)*

CIRCULAR PAPER PUNCH *(EK Success)*

MONOADHESIVE *(Tombow USA)*

CHIPBOARD DISKS *(Bazzill)*

BRAYER

SUPPLIES
to Complete the Project

CARDSTOCK

PATTERNED PAPER *(Iota)*

CHIPBOARD LETTERS *(Heidi Swapp)*

SONGWRITER FONT *(Autumn Leaves)*

DIE-CUT PHOTO CORNERS *(QuicKutz)*

UHU GLUE STICK

cousins

HOW WE BECAME DOG PEOPLE

by Tena

❊ TECHNIQUE ❊ *Using a transparency in stamp placement*

How we became

DOG People

PEPPER

How one little puppy
Managed to wrap a
Whole family around
Her little paw!

LITTLE BITT

PEPPER

KS OLD

hood

Our family has gone through a major transformation in the last year and a half: We have turned into Dog People. Funny as it sounds, we were always the type of folks who found it ridiculous the way some people treated their pets like family and let their world revolve around their animals—but now we *are* those people! Since adopting our dog, Pepper, I have been wanting to do a project telling the story of how she **joined our family and changed our lives.** Because Pepper loves to wear things out and chew on them, I decided this book should look weathered and loved, so I chose corrugated cardboard for the pages. I also altered my photos the old-fashioned way: with my art supplies!

chronicling **tip**

MINI BOOKS ARE THE PERFECT FORMAT FOR SHARING STORIES THAT MAY BE HARD TO TELL ON A SINGLE SCRAPBOOK PAGE. YOU CAN ALSO CUSTOMIZE YOUR BOOK TO FIT THE SUBJECT MATTER, UNLIKE A SCRAPBOOK PAGE THAT MUST BLEND IN WITH THE REST OF THE SCRAPBOOK ALBUM.

pets

Stamp on transparency

Stamp onto a transparency sheet using the ink and stamp you plan to use on your photo.

Place stamped transparency over photo

Place the stamped transparency sheet over the photo to decide upon the placement of the stamp.

Stamp photo

When you're satisfied with the placement, remove the transparency and stamp the photo.

Ink edges of photo

Apply ink to the edges of the photo by pressing each edge into an ink pad.

Distress photo with sandpaper

Use a fine-grain sandpaper to sand the photo. The fine grain removes color without damaging the photo paper.

tip YOU MAY ALSO ALTER YOUR PHOTOS BY APPLYING ACRYLIC PAINT WITH A FOAM BRUSH OR BRISTLE BRUSH. JUST MAKE SURE TO USE THE LEAST AMOUNT OF PAINT POSSIBLE TO AVOID OVERWETTING YOUR PHOTO, WHICH CAN CAUSE THE PHOTO TO RIPPLE OR THE PHOTO INK TO BLEED.

AS WE GREW MORE ATTACHED TO PEPPER WE NOTICED OURSELVES EXHIBITING ALL THE DOG-PEOPLE BEHAVIORS WE HAD ALWAYS FOUND RIDICULOUS IN OTHER PEOPLE. WE TALKED TO HER IN BABY-TALK. WE MADE UP NICK-NAMES FOR HER, WE TALKED ABOUT HER LIKE ONE OF THE FAMILY, WE CONSTANTLY TOLD EACH OTHER THAT SHE WAS THE BEST LOOKING SCHNAUZER IN THE WORLD, WE EVEN TALKED TO HER ON THE PHONE WHEN WE WERE OUT OF TOWN. THIS LITTLE DOGGIE HAD US IN THE PALM OF HER PAW!

construction **notes**

I constructed this handmade book with four cardstock pages of graduated lengths. I covered the front of each page with corrugated cardboard, leaving a 1" (3cm) binding edge on the left side, and backed each page with thin chipboard by using a glue stick to adhere the layers, then brayering to secure them. Using a standard hole punch, I punched two holes in the binding edge, then tied the pages together with twine.

YOU'RE STILL THE ONE | by Carol

you're STILL the ONE

OUR
LOVE
IS
GOING
GOLD

Being married to my college sweetheart, Vern, for more than twenty-nine years **is a joy and a pleasure.** I created this book, based on the lyrics of the song "You're Still the One," as a celebration of our love and commitment. This book started out as a spiral-bound journal that I transformed to look like an old building with a window. The application of gesso and alabaster fresco flakes added to the feeling of age. Vern's photo was then resized and altered to fit behind the window. I love the depth and the feeling of being drawn into the cover. For my favorite page, I used micro folders to journal about our relationship. You could apply this technique to your own tribute book, or to any number of other projects.

SUPPLIES
for the Technique

MICRO FILE FOLDERS *(DMD)*

PAINTBRUSH

GESSO *(Golden)*

INK PADS

MAKEUP SPONGE

STAMPS *(Green Pepper Press)*

AWL

BLACK WRITING MARKER

COARSE THREAD

SUPPLIES
to Complete the Project

ALBUM *(Mysticpress.com)*

WINDOW *(Renaissance Art)*

FLASHCARD LETTERS *(7gypsies)*

RUB-ONS *(Chartpak)*

LETTER TILES *(Westrim)*

BRACKETS *(Quickutz)*

FRESCO FLAKES *(Stewart Gill)*

DIE-CUT PUNCTUATION *(QuicKutz)*

ACRYLIC PAINT *(Delta)*

WAXED NYLON BINDING THREAD
(Books By Hand)

UHU GLUE STICK

BRAYER

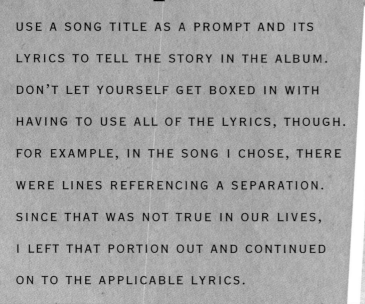

chronicling **tip**

USE A SONG TITLE AS A PROMPT AND ITS LYRICS TO TELL THE STORY IN THE ALBUM. DON'T LET YOURSELF GET BOXED IN WITH HAVING TO USE ALL OF THE LYRICS, THOUGH. FOR EXAMPLE, IN THE SONG I CHOSE, THERE WERE LINES REFERENCING A SEPARATION. SINCE THAT WAS NOT TRUE IN OUR LIVES, I LEFT THAT PORTION OUT AND CONTINUED ON TO THE APPLICABLE LYRICS.

• husband

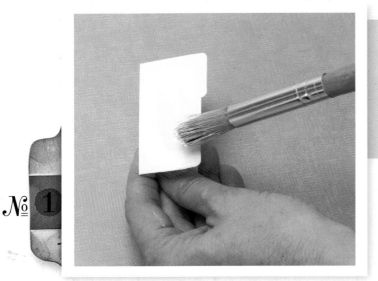

Paint file folders with gesso

Determine the number of file folders you
need to spell out your word or phrase.
Drybrush the micro file folders with white
gesso. Allow it to dry.

No. 1

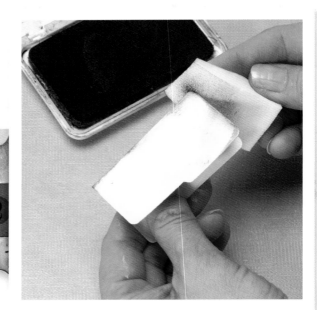

Antique edges of folders

Apply brown ink to a sponge and rub the inked
sponge along the edges of the file folders to create
an antiqued look.

No. 2

Stamp on letters

Stamp a letter onto the front of each micro file
folder with black ink to spell out the sentiment of
your choice.

No. 3

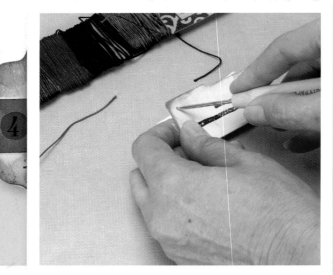

No. 4

Poke holes in micro file folders

Use an awl to poke a hole in the top left corner of
the front flap of each micro file folder. Write a little
story inside each folder.

Tie on string

Cut small pieces of coarse thread and string them through the holes in the mini file folders. Knot each piece of thread and trim the ends as desired. Journal the "story" inside each micro folder.

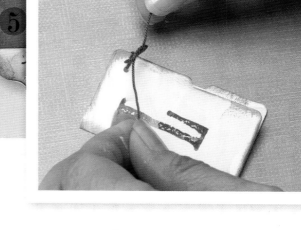

construction notes

This book came with a variety of inserts, such as tags and transparent and vellum pockets. Modifying photos and adding journaling to these various surfaces added a fun dimension to the project.

BELONGING | by Carol

The need to belong is one of the most basic human needs, just above physical health and safety. Almost everyone belongs to some sort of group: clubs, churches, online communities, support groups, sports teams—the list goes on. **Family is one of the most** basic and **important groups.**

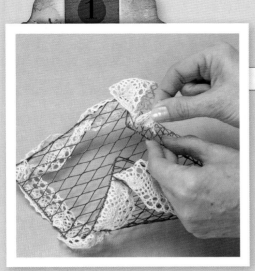

Weave wide ribbon

Weave a wide, lacy ribbon under and over the wire at the top of the cone, folding the ribbon in half if desired.

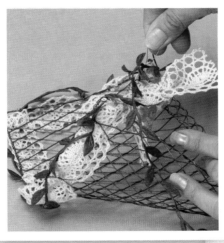

Weave narrow ribbon

Weave a piece of silk ribbon with leaves under and over the wire at the top of the cone, making sure the ribbon is visible on top of the wider ribbon.

Sew on buttons

Use a sewing needle and thread to secure the ribbon ends together at the front of the cone. Sew up and down through the button holes and the ribbon several times to secure.

construction **notes**

I created this project to hang in my studio to remind myself of what it means to belong to my family. I captured my thoughts about family on die-cut tags and tucked them into this cone.

SUPPLIES
for the Technique

WIRE CONE *(Stampington)*

RIBBON *(May Arts)*

NEEDLE AND THREAD

BUTTONS

SUPPLIES
to Complete the Project

FIBERS

DIE CUT TAGS *(AccuCut)*

TACKY GLUE

chronicling **tip**

WIRE CONES MAKE GREAT GIFTS. CONSIDER GIVING ONE AS A WEDDING SHOWER GIFT, FILLED WITH HAND-WRITTEN TAGS EXPRESSING EACH ATTENDEE'S WISHES FOR THE BRIDE. FILL ONE WITH TAGS GIVING ADVICE TO A NEW MOM AND PRESENT IT AT A BABY SHOWER. OR, HANG THE CONE FROM A DOORKNOB, THE KNOB OF AN ARMOIRE, THE CORNER OF A MIRROR OR A BULLETIN BOARD. FILL IT WITH PRAYERS, VERSES OR FAVORITE QUOTES.

My daughter, Alyssa, is going on sixteen, and **so many things in her life are changing.** In the past month she got her driver's permit and applied for her first paying job. We have even started to talk about colleges and careers. Reality has set in: This girl is almost grown! This layout commemorates where we are today and what we are on the edge of. I chose the graffiti style of writing because it reminds me of Alyssa's printing as well as the writing on the T-shirts she always wears, and this technique was the perfect way to bring the style to life on the page.

SUPPLIES
for the Technique

PATTERNED PAPER *(7gypsies)*

UHU GLUE STICK

CHIPBOARD

BRAYER

CLEAR EMBOSSING PEN *(Zig)*

CLEAR EMBOSSING POWDER *(Ranger)*

HEAT GUN FOR EMBOSSING

FOAM PAINTBRUSHES

ACRYLIC PAINT *(FolkArt)*

SOFT CLOTH

GLAZE PEN *(Sakura)*

CARDSTOCK

ELECTRONIC FUSES

SUPPLIES
to Complete the Project

E-6000 GLUE

TWO-SIDED TAPE *(Magic Scraps)*

chronicling **tip**

USING EMBOSSING PENS AND POWDER OR GLAZE PENS TO GIVE YOUR HANDWRITTEN JOURNALING A RAISED APPEARANCE IS A GREAT TECHNIQUE TO USE ON ART SURFACES THAT MIGHT NOT ACCEPT TRADITIONAL ARCHIVAL INKS. GLAZE PENS CAN ALSO BE USED ON PHOTOS TO CREATE A RAISED FINISH TO HAND JOURNALING.

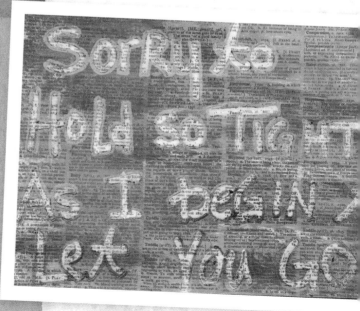

daughter

Mount background paper on chipboard

Apply the glue stick to the back of your background paper and adhere it to a piece of chipboard. The sturdy chipboard makes the paper strong enough to support paint and embossing.

№ 2

Journal onto paper with embossing pen

Use a clear embossing pen with a chisel or wide tip to handwrite journaling onto the patterned paper.

№ 3

Sprinkle on embossing powder

Sprinkle clear embossing powder over all of the still-wet journaling.

№ 4

Heat-set embossing powder

With a heat gun, set the embossing powder. Move the heat gun back and forth above the journaling, keeping it a few inches away to avoid scorching the paper.

№ 5

Paint over journaling

Use a paintbrush to apply acrylic paint over the embossed journaling.

№ 6

Wipe away paint

Directly after applying the paint, use a soft cloth to wipe away the still-wet paint from the embossed letters. Embossed writing resists paint, so it wipes off easily. You do not need to apply much pressure with the cloth.

№ 7

Outline journaling with glaze pen

Use a glaze pen to trace around the outside of all of the embossed letters.

construction **notes**

Once your embossed journaling piece is complete, cut away the appropriate amount of chipboard to reveal your photo beneath the embossed chipboard layer. Adhere the photo to the back of the chipboard, then mount it on the background cardstock and reinforce the back with chipboard again for support. Use electronic fuses as embellishments along the left side, adhering them between the layers of chipboard and cardstock with E-6000 glue.

IT'S A BLOG WORLD | by Tena

I created this little "techno-looking" book to **celebrate the connections** I have made through the world of blogging. This modern, metal store-bought photo album turned out to be a fantastic mini scrapbook. I created the pages using cardstock cut to the size of the photo sleeves, then mounted embellishments and screen-printed blog entries onto the cardstock.

Print out images

Select the photo or screen image you would like to apply to the surface of your metal project. Resize the image using your photo-editing tools to match the surface dimensions of your project. Print the images onto an adhesive-backed transparency, being sure to use the transparency setting on your printer. Trim the images if necessary.

SUPPLIES
for the Technique

BRUSHED ALUMINUM ALBUM CASE AND PHOTO SLEEVES *(Umbra)*, OR OTHER METAL SURFACE OF YOUR CHOICE

ELECTRONIC IMAGE OF YOUR CHOICE

PRINTER

ADHESIVE TRANPARENCY SHEETS *(Grafix)*

BRAYER

SUPPLIES
to Complete the Project

CARDSTOCK

MINI BRADS

FAUX KEYBOARD KEYS *(Creative Imaginations)*

DIE-CUT TABS *(QuicKutz)*

LETTER DIE CUTS *(QuicKutz)*

RUB-ON ACCENTS *(Heidi Swapp)*

MONOADHESIVE TAPE *(Tombow USA)*

E-6000 GLUE

Adhere stickers to box

Carefully place the stickers where you'd like them to go on the box. Peel away the backing and adhere the stickers.

chronicling **tip**

MUCH OF THE JOURNALING AND PAGES USED IN MY BLOG BOOK WERE PRINTED DIRECTLY FROM MY BLOG ENTRIES. PRINT OUT YOUR ENTRIES ON A REGULAR BASIS AND FILE THEM IN A FOLDER. MANY TIMES I FIND THAT THE THINGS I BLOG ABOUT ARE THE SAME THINGS THAT INSPIRE MY MEMORY ART PROJECTS, SO THE JOURNALING AND PHOTOS COME IN HANDY AND SAVE ME LOTS OF TIME!

Brayer over stickers

Brayer over all stickers to smooth away any air bubbles.

tip ADHESIVE-BACKED TRANSPARENCIES ARE ALSO A GREAT PRODUCT TO USE WHEN LAYERING TEXT OR PHOTOS ON ANY PAPER ARTS PROJECT OR SCRAPBOOKING LAYOUT. THEY ARE LIGHTWEIGHT AND READY TO STICK TO YOUR PROJECT SURFACE.

me

SIT TALL IN THE
SADDLE OF LIFE
by Carol

❧ TECHNIQUE ❧ *Creating a shabby frame with corrugated cardboard*

You have accomplished much

You have exercised discipline

You set goals & go for them

You've had triumphs & disappointments

Sit tall, absorb, learn & grow

Sit TALL
IN THE
SADDLE
OF life

I am a quote fanatic. When I saw this phrase on a greeting card one day, I just knew I needed to create a project around it—which is not hard to do in our household, where horses play an important role and saddles sometimes reign supreme in our family room! I thought about Ashley's **growth in character,** *sportsmanship* **and understanding of life**—all of which have come through in her riding pursuits. Ashley and her pony have grown up together, and it's through this connection that many of her life lessons have been learned. This photo was taken at Ashley's first endurance ride. This shabby frame is a perfect complement to the rustic image.

SUPPLIES
for the Technique

CORRUGATED CARDBOARD

TACKY GLUE

FRAME *(Provo Craft)*

BRISTLE BRUSH

GESSO *(Golden)*

IVORY AND RUST-COLORED ACRYLIC PAINTS *(Plaid)*

SPONGE

SUPPLIES
to Complete the Project

RUBBER STAMPS *(Stampotique, Green Pepper Press)*

NOTCH MAKER *(BasicGrey)*

BRADS *(Karen Foster Design)*

RIBBON *(American Crafts)*

LABELS *(Dymo)*

TICKET

O-RING

MASK *(Heidi Swapp)*

chronicling **tip**

USE A QUOTE AS A PROMPT FOR A TITLE OR FOR THE THEME OF YOUR PROJECT. ADD VARIETY AND INTEREST BY USING DIFFERENT FONTS OR SEVERAL SIZES OF LETTERS TO SHOWCASE THE QUOTE.

children

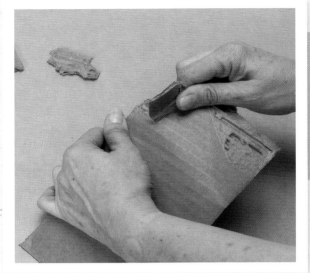

Tear up cardboard

Tear up a piece of corrugated cardboard into small pieces with irregular edges. Some pieces may be thicker and some may be thinner. Different thicknesses of cardboard pieces will add dimension to the frame.

Adhere cardboard pieces to frame

Use tacky glue to adhere the pieces of cardboard to the frame in a random fashion. You may group several pieces close together and leave more space between other pieces.

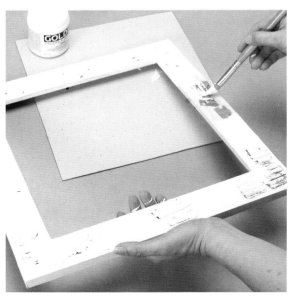

Paint frame with gesso and ivory paint

Use a bristle brush to paint white gesso over the entire frame, covering the cardboard pieces completely. Allow the gesso to dry, then drybrush over the gesso with ivory paint. Some of the gesso should show through the ivory paint. Allow the paint to dry.

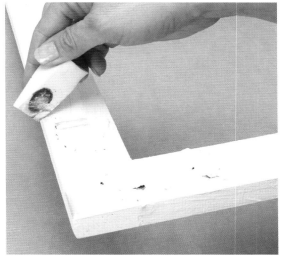

Sponge on rust-colored paint

Squirt a small amount of rust-colored paint onto
a sponge and apply it sparingly to different spots
on the frame to create an antiqued look.

you have accomplished much

you have exercised discipline

you set goals & go for them

You've had triumphs & disappointments

Sit tall, absorb, learn & grow

construction notes

Select a photo that has some
"empty" space so you have
room to add words. Enlarge it
to fit inside the frame, then
add journaling.

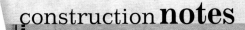

MICHAEL'S ART | by Tena

My son, Michael, is a **budding writer and artist**. For as long as I can remember, he has been fascinated with superheroes and comic books. A couple of years ago he started creating his own comic books, complete with original characters. To showcase his art, I decided to frame some of my favorite drawings from Michael's first comic book creation, "Bubbleman." A photo mat adorned with stickers featuring more of his art ties it all together.

Create stickers

Select the artwork to make into stickers and scan it into your computer. Adjust the size of the artwork to fit the project, then print it onto adhesive transparency sheets.

DIGITAL IMAGE OF THE ARTWORK OF YOUR CHOICE

PRINTER

ADHESIVE TRANSPARENCY SHEETS *(Grafix)*

SCISSORS

TWEEZERS

PHOTO MAT

BRAYER

SUPPLIES
to Complete the Project

ACRYLIC PAINT AND GLAZE *(FolkArt, Delta, Heidi Swapp)*

ART TAPE

MONOADHESIVE TAPE *(Tombow USA)*

Cut out stickers

Cut as close as possible to the artwork lines to avoid showing sticker edges and fingerprints.

Adhere stickers to photo mat

Peel the backing away from each sticker (use clean hands for best results) and use tweezers to apply them to the mat (to avoid fingerprints). Repeat until all the stickers are in place. Use a brayer to roll over the stickers to squeeze out any air bubbles.

chronicling tip

CONSIDER INCORPORATING HAND-DRAWN ART, EPHEMERA OR HANDWRITTEN NOTES INTO YOUR ARTWORK. THESE PERSONAL ITEMS CAN BE ALTERED USING YOUR SCANNER AND IMAGE TRANSFER PRODUCTS. THEN SIMPLY APPLY THEM TO THE SURFACE OF YOUR PROJECT.

son

It's great to be a girl! The girls in my family have always outnumbered the boys (yay!). Both of my parents had more sisters than brothers, and females also prevailed among my cousins. It seemed fitting to create a book about the girls (though I couldn't include them all because of the constraints of space).

I filled my book with photos that reflected the personality of each individual female I had decided to include. I also added journaling and **funny anecdotes about the female contingent in our family**. The stamped, embossed metal cover gives the book a unique look.

SUPPLIES
for the Technique

CRAFTER'S PEWTER (*MercArt*)

STAMPS (*FontWerks*)

SOLVENT BLACK INK PAD (*StazOn*)

PIECE OF SUEDE OR CRAFTER'S FOAM

STYLUS OR OTHER METAL EMBOSSING TOOL

PLAIN PAPER

LIGHTWEIGHT PLASTER OR MODELING PASTE (*optional*)

CHIPBOARD

SCISSORS

HEAVY-DUTY GLUE, SUCH AS THICK DESIGNER TACKY GLUE OR E-6000

PAINTBRUSH

WHITE GESSO (*Golden*)

ACRYLIC PAINT IN A COORDINATING COLOR (*Plaid*)

SUPPLIES
to Complete the Project

FOLDER (*Avery Dennison*)

CARDSTOCK ACCORDION BOOK (*Bazzill*)

PAPER (*SEI*)

BUTTONS (*SEI*)

BRADS (*American Crafts*)

RIBBON (*May Arts*)

FABRIC FLOWERS (*Primamarketing*)

FLOWER PUNCH (*Paper Shapers*)

PUNCTUATION (*QuicKutz*)

PAINTBRUSH

AWL

SCISSORS

chronicling **tip**

A BOOK LIKE THIS WOULD MAKE A FABULOUS TRAVEL JOURNAL. THE POCKETS PROVIDE A GREAT PLACE TO STORE MENUS, TICKETS, BROCHURES AND OTHER TRAVEL MEMENTOS. MAKE YOUR JOURNAL IN ADVANCE, AND IT WILL HELP YOU STAY ORGANIZED THROUGHOUT YOUR TRIP.

sisters

Stamp onto metal

Stamp the title of your book onto the metal piece with solvent black ink, such as StazOn.

Emboss letters

Place the metal piece faceup on a piece of suede or crafter's foam. Trace around the edges of the stamped letters with a stylus or embossing tool using medium pressure, placing a piece of paper between your hand and the metal to prevent smearing the ink.

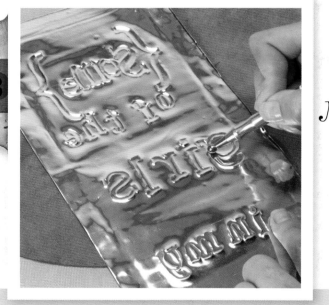

Deboss letters

Flip the piece of metal over so it is facedown on the suede or crafter's foam. Run the stylus over the space between the outlines, causing the letters to pop out on the front side. If desired, you may apply lightweight plaster or modeling paste to the spaces in the back of the metal piece to prevent the raised portions of the front from compressing. Allow the paste to dry.

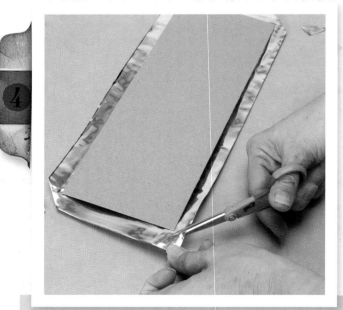

Miter corners of crafter's metal

Cut a piece of chipboard about ½" (1cm) smaller on all sides than the metal piece. Lay the metal piece facedown on your work surface, and adhere the chipboard in the center with a heavy-duty glue. Cut away all the corners of the crafter's metal.

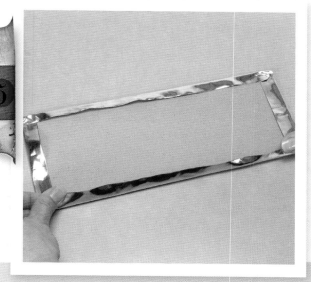

Secure crafter's metal to chipboard

Roll the edges of the metal from front to back. Glue is not necessary as the metal holds its place. Compress the corners if the metal feels sharp.

Finish the cover

To finish the cover, lightly paint over the surface of the metal with white gesso. When the gesso is dry, brush a coordinating acrylic paint around the metal edges. Use a heavy-duty glue to apply the metal piece to the book cover (or project of your choice).

belongs to a particular place; a female sweet-heart.

StRikE a PoSt

construction notes

The structure of this funky mini book is a project folder found in most office supply stores. I accordion-folded the folder so there were front and back covers as well as four interior panels on which to create. The great thing about this folder is that there are pockets on each inside page. This allowed me to add cascading tags in one pocket and a tall, skinny accordion-folded mini book in another pocket, thus greatly expanding my space.

TWENTY-SIX YEARS
OF FRIENDSHIP

by Tena

❖ TECHNIQUE ❖ *Using acrylic paint to create texture on canvas*

I count myself lucky to have a best girlfriend, particularly one who also lives in my home state of Arizona. My friendship with Laurie is one of my most important connections outside of my family. She has been there for every important event in my life. She **makes me laugh, inspires me and picks me up** when I am at my lowest. We met when we were at Michigan State University. I ended up finishing my last two years of college in Arizona, and when I moved away I hoped we'd stay close friends. The night before I left, we played the song from which the lyrics showcased in this piece are taken. I have always marveled at how true and how prophetic those words have come to be. I know twenty-five years from now, we'll still be taking pictures like the one showcased by the painted canvas in this project.

SUPPLIES
for the Technique

WHITE CANVAS *(Canvas Concepts)*

FOAM BRUSHES

ACRYLIC PAINT

STAINING MEDIUM

PAINTBRUSH

SOFT CLOTH *(optional)*

PAINT MASK *(Heidi Swapp)*

BRAYER

PATTERN BUILDER *(Delta)*

PALETTE KNIFE

SUPPLIES
to Complete the Project

ARTIST'S CANVAS PAPER

PATTERNED PAPER *(Earth Spice by Captured Elements)*

PAINTED BACKGROUND PAPER *(sketchpad paper by Canson)*

PHOTO *(the photo used here was taken by Kim Kwan)*

CHIPBOARD NUMBERS/LETTERS *(Heidi Swapp)*

FABRIC *(Michael Miller)*

GEL MEDIUM *(Golden)*

TWO-SIDED PHOTO STICKY TAPE

E-6000 GLUE

JOURNALING PEN *(Sakura)*

chronicling **tip**

ANOTHER WAY TO USE TEXTURE PRODUCTS TO CREATE DIMENSION IS TO APPLY THE TEXTURED PAINT TO YOUR CRAFT SURFACE, AND THEN STAMP INTO IT WITH IMAGE OR ALPHABET STAMPS.

friends

Paint canvas

Use a foam brush to apply a thin layer of acrylic paint to the canvas. Cover the entire canvas, but allow the white to peak through a little.

Stain edges of canvas

Mix equal parts of acrylic paint and staining medium. Use a soft cloth or paintbrush to lightly apply the stain mixture to the edges of the canvas to create depth and dimension. If the mixture begins to dry out, you can refresh it by mixing in a bit of water.

Adhere mask

Lay the mask on one edge of the canvas and brayer over it to adhere it well to the canvas.

tip MASKS CAN ALSO BE USED WITH INK, SPRAY PAINTS, CHALKS AND OTHER ART MEDIUMS TO CREATE INTERESTING RESISTED IMAGES ON YOUR ART PROJECTS.

Apply thick layer of paint

Mix equal parts of acrylic paint and texture builder medium. Apply a thick layer of paint over the mask with a palette knife. Gently lift the mask off after the paint has been applied to reveal the resisted image on the canvas. Allow plenty of time for the paint to dry completely. In some more humid climates, the drying process may take a full twenty-four hours.

Add finishing touches with complementary color

Once the paint is fully dry, carefully pull up the mask. With a small paintbrush, apply a complementary color of paint inside the outline left by the mask.

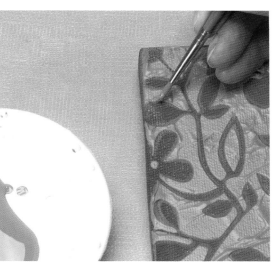

construction **notes**

To finish construction of this wall canvas, a photo mat was created using artist's canvas paper that was painted with acrylic paint and layered with patterned paper, and these papers were adhered to the surface of the canvas using gel medium. The photo was adhered to the mat using two-sided photo sticky tape. The chipboard letters used for the title were painted with acrylic paint to match the other elements on the canvas and adhered with E-6000 glue.

HAVE AND HOLD | by Carol

❃ TECHNIQUE ❃ *Creating an image transfer with a Polaroid emulsion lift*

HAVe

&

HOLD

touch is the most intimate of connections

it passes along strength

it provides warmth & comfort

Baby Fuller & Grandpa

I love to see **tender moments captured by the camera**, and there's nothing as tender as the first days of an infant's life. This photo captures Baby Fuller holding tight to his grandfather's thumb. What a marvelous connection. The image prompted me to build this piece around touch, the most intimate of human connections. I showcased this simple photo by creating a Polaroid emulsion lift with it.

SUPPLIES
for the Technique

POLAROID IMAGE

TWO PLASTIC CONTAINERS, BIG ENOUGH TO FIT YOUR POLAROID IMAGE, FILLED WITH WATER

MICROWAVE, HOT POT OR STOVE

THERMOMETER

PLASTIC TONGS

WATERCOLOR PAPER

BRAYER

PAPER TOWELS

TIMER

WATERCOLOR CRAYONS *(Staedtler)*

SUPPLIES
to Complete the Project

PAPER *(7gypsies)*

RUB-ON LETTERS *(Autumn Leaves)*

FLOURISH DIE CUTS *(QuicKutz)*

INK *(Ranger)*

chronicling tip

USE YOUR OWN HANDWRITING. WHEN A PROJECT DEALS WITH INTIMATE CONNECTIONS, JOURNALING IN YOUR OWN HAND APPEARS MORE IN KEEPING WITH THE SUBJECT MATTER THAN THE SOMEWHAT MORE CLINICAL FEEL OF COMPUTER JOURNALING.

• children

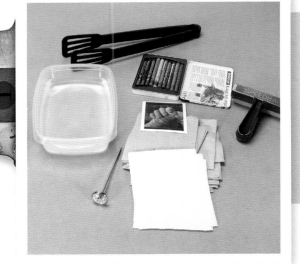

Gather supplies

Since this is a time-sensitive process, it's a good idea to gather all your supplies before you begin. You'll need two shallow containers of water, one heated to 160°F (71°C) and the other left at room temperature. In addition, gather some tongs for maneuvering the photo, a thermometer, watercolor paper, a brayer, paper towels, a timer, watercolor crayons and, of course, the Polaroid image.

Immerse Polaroid in hot water

Use the thermometer to check that your water is 160°F (71°C). I recommend starting with water at 180°F (82°C) to allow for cooling off. Immerse the Polaroid faceup in the water for four minutes. The image bubbles a little when it's time to remove it.

Immerse Polaroid in room-temperature water

Use a pair of tongs to remove the print, and place it faceup in the room-temperature water tray.

Slide watercolor paper under emulsion

Lightly push the emulsion from the edges of the print, being careful not to allow the emulsion to fold over onto itself, and use light pressure with your fingernails so the thin film does not tear. When the film is fully separated from the backing, remove the backing and allow the film to float in the water. Begin to carefully slide the watercolor paper under the film.

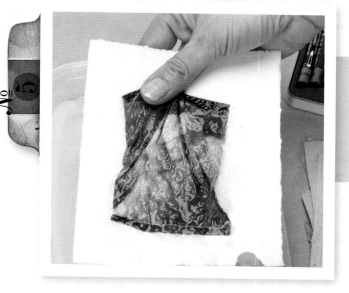

Transfer film to watercolor paper

Gently and slowly slide the watercolor paper fully under the film. When you're satisfied with the placement, lift the transfer from the water.

tip TO CREATE THE POLAROID IMAGE YOU'LL NEED FOR THE EMULSION LIFT PROCESS, EXPOSE YOUR PRINT OR SLIDE ONTO POLAROID INSTANT FILM (TYPE 669, 59, 559 OR 809) WITH A DAYLAB OR INSTANT SLIDE PRINTER. PROCESS THE FILM PER THE INSTRUCTIONS AND LET IT DRY COMPLETELY (OR FORCE IT TO DRY WITH A HAIR DRYER).

Adhere image to paper

Use your fingers to gently spread out the film, smoothing away any wrinkles. Starting at the center and moving out toward the edges, use the brayer to remove excess water. Allow the transfer to dry completely. When dry, the film will adhere to the paper without glue.

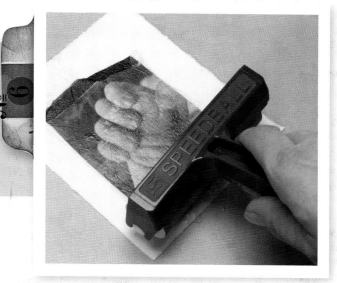

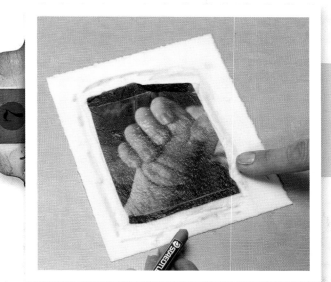

Add watercolor crayon border

When the transfer is dry, color around the edges of the image with watercolor crayons. Apply plain water over the markings to blend them.

tip WHEN YOU ARE MANIPULATING THE TRANSFER WITH YOUR FINGERS (STEPS FIVE AND SIX), IF YOU DON'T LIKE THE RESULTS ON YOUR FIRST TRY, YOU MAY START OVER BY IMMERSING THE IMAGE IN THE ROOM-TEMPERATURE WATER BATH. SIMPLY REMOVE THE IMAGE AGAIN AND CONTINUE TO MANIPULATE IT UNTIL YOU ACHIEVE YOUR DESIRED EFFECT.

OUR FAVORITE PLACES

by Carol

❊ TECHNIQUE ❊

Transferring an image with blender markers

One of our mutual family interests is travel. As often as possible, when we're out of town we try to stay at small bed-and-breakfast establishments rather than hotels. It's fun to talk to the hosts, who are more than willing to give the locals' insider perspective on tourist attractions and events. We always ask them where the locals like to eat, and we've yet to be disappointed with a recommendation. Vern, Ashley and I enjoy **the experience of connecting with people** in other parts of our country and the world. This project commemorates our adventures by displaying transferred photos from our travels.

SUPPLIES
for the Technique

MANILA TAGBOARD OR WHITE ARTIST TRADING CARDS

CORNER ROUNDER

WALNUT INK *(7gypsies)* OR LIGHT BROWN INK PAD

DIGITAL IMAGES

PRINTER

PHOTO TRANSFER PAPER

XYLENE BLENDER PEN *(Chartpak)*

BONE FOLDER

SUPPLIES
to Complete the Project

TORSO *(DCC)*

MAP PAPER *(Cavallini Papers)*

SHIPPING TAG *(Avery Dennison)*

MAP TAPE *(Heidi Swapp)*

NARROW TWILL

VINTAGE CRYSTAL DOORKNOB

VINTAGE-STYLE UPHOLSTERY TACKS

MATTE GEL MEDIUM *(Golden)*

E-6000 GLUE

chronicling **tip**

IMAGE-TRANSFERRED PHOTOS MAY BE DIRECTLY APPLIED TO THE TORSO TO RESEMBLE PAPIER MÂCHÉ. IT IS RECOMMENDED THAT THE IMAGES BE SPRAYED WITH A MATTE SEALER PRIOR TO APPLYING ANY MOISTURE SO THE IMAGES DON'T SMEAR. ADD A BIT OF HAND JOURNALING WITH AN "ALL-SURFACE" TYPE OF PEN. FOR EXTRA FUN, HAVE YOUR TRAVELING COMPANIONS ADD THEIR THOUGHTS AND IMPRESSIONS.

family

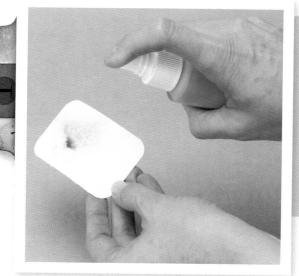

Create tags

Since most premade cards and tags are white and glossy (which is not desirable for the vintage look of this project), I created my own with manila-colored tagboard (but you might use artist trading cards instead). My cards are 2 ⅛" x 3 ⅛" (5cm × 8cm). Round the corners of each card with a corner rounder. Lightly spray each card with walnut ink, or color them using a light brown ink pad. Allow the ink to dry.

Make copies of images

Digitally resize the photos of your choice to fit the cards. Print black-and-white toner-based copies of all of the images onto photo transfer paper. It's a good idea to print several copies of each photo to allow for errors in the transfer process.

Apply blender marker to back of image

Place an image facedown onto a tag. Apply the xylene blender pen to the entire back of the image, totally covering it with solvent.

Burnish image onto tag

Use a bone folder to burnish over the entire back of the image, making sure to give all areas equal pressure.

tip IF YOU ARE TRANSFERRING A LARGE IMAGE, IT HELPS TO CLIP THE PHOTOCOPY TO THE RECEIVING PAPER TO HOLD IT IN PLACE. YOU MAY HAVE TO APPLY THE SOLVENT SEVERAL TIMES SO IT DOESN'T DRY TOO QUICKLY.

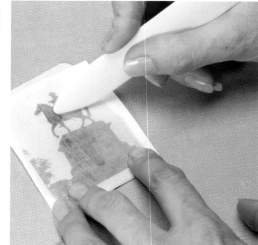

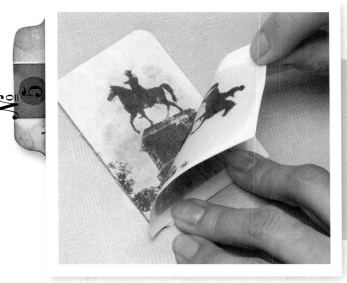

Peel away photocopy to reveal transferred image

Peel back the photocopy at one corner to check the transfer process. If the image is fully transferred, remove the photocopy and discard it immediately. Because some of the solvent remains on the photocopy until it dries, the image may transfer to other surfaces, such as tabletops.

construction **notes**

The base for this project is a papier mâché torso. I tore a parent sheet of map paper into pieces of various sizes and shapes and adhered them to the torso with gel medium. I then punched a hole in the top of the torso and inserted a vintage crystal doorknob. I used E-6000 glue to make sure that the knob would be sturdy (in case anyone decided to lift the project by the knob!). I then added vintage upholstery tacks and a tag around the knob. The skirt was created by adding tags to a piece of twill, wrapping it around the waist of the torso and holding it in place with upholstery tacks.

sweet
daughter
KELLY ANDERSON

I found this white frame in a clearance bin for twenty-five cents because it was missing the back and glass front. I liked the grid structure and decided to make a collage for my daughter's room. This can stand by itself, may be leaned up on a shelf or could also be hung from a ribbon on the wall.

to teach
is to touch a life
LAURIE STAMAS

I have taught Sunday School for about fifteen years now, but I had never done a layout sharing that important part of my life. Each year, the kids in my class bring me so much joy, and it is always hard when the end of the year rolls around. This year at graduation, my daughter Alexia took this photo of me with my class. I decided to use a familiar saying for my title because it seemed so appropriate: To teach *is* to touch a life forever. I'm just not sure whose life has been touched more—the students' or mine.

sweet baby
madeline

KELLY ANDERSON

Motherhood is an amazing new experience. I can't believe how much my daughter is changing each month, and I wanted to create a book that captured the important details of each month of her young life without undertaking an overwhelming project. I decided to transform a CD pack into an unbound book to record my baby's first two years. Each CD reflects a month and is designed with photos and journaling about milestones, developments and events. And the project is manageable for a busy new mama like me because I have to create only one CD per month.

right here **right now**

JESSIE BALDWIN

I learned to read with Dr. Seuss, and my mom was thoughtful enough to save several of these books from my childhood. Twenty-six years later, my daughter, Violet, is learning to read in her kindergarten class. When she pulled out an old, familiar, orange-covered book, my heart caught in my throat. We sat down together and Violet read to me from my very own copy of Dr. Seuss's *Green Eggs and Ham.* I am so very glad my husband took pictures of this historic moment.

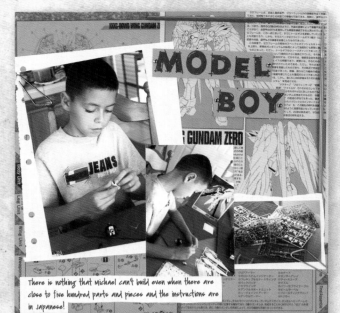

There is nothing that Michael can't build even when there are close to five hundred parts and pieces and the instructions are in Japanese!

model **boy**
TENA SPRENGER

The men in my family are gifted when it comes to putting things together, and the gene was definitely passed on to my son, Michael! Last Christmas he received a fancy model that had a high level of difficulty and more parts than similar models he had built. Michael and his dad designated a weekend to build the model and upon opening the box discovered that its instructions were in Japanese! Fortunately, they were up for the challenge!

A FRIEND IS SOMEONE WHO KNOWS ALL ABOUT YOU, BUT LIKES YOU ANYWAY.

fairy **girlfriend**
KATHERINE BROOKS

I have always been inspired by those adorable vintage-looking fairies that artists create, but I love taking a different approach by creating my fairies from current photos rather than older photos. I created this canvas of one of my best girlfriends to show the circle of our friendship, what connects us to each other.

JUST THE FIVE OF US TOGETHER SO MANY HAPPY MEMORIES HERE IN OUR DESERT HOME
Summer 2006

cherish **now**
HEIDI SWAPP

For five years, it's just been the five of us in the Swapp family. But this is about to change as we welcome a new member to our family next month. I had some family photos taken on Mother's Day this year, as I was contemplating the drastic change about to happen to our family dynamics. I wanted to convey that with time comes change and growth. I love the imagery of clocks as a reminder of the precious nature of time.

sisters
LAURIE STAMAS

When I saw this unique frame at a local store, I just knew I needed to create something with it. I loved how photos were intended to hang from the dowels with the little mini clips. I decided to take some new photos of my daughters to use for this project and have them dress in a color scheme that would match the room where I wanted to put the finished piece. I love how the photos really capture my girls' personalities. Looking at them made the journaling I added come easily.

california **adventure**
CAROL WINGERT

My daughter, Ashley, has been best friends with Elizabeth for twelve years. The girls spent months planning their first girls-only trip, doing research and agonizing over their destination, before finally deciding on Disneyland. While both had been there with family, this was going to be different because they did the planning and the paying! They had an incredible time, and to commemorate the trip I created a magnetic memo board out of a cookie sheet. My biggest challenge was choosing photos: Between them they took almost four hundred pictures!

Forever Remembered

All of us have special people in our recent or distant past who have made impressions on us that will last a lifetime, people who have altered and shaped the courses of our lives. One of the best examples in my own life is my Grandma Dahl. I truly believe that my obsession with reading is a direct result of her positive influence. It started with Grandma reading books to me—as many as I wanted—and evolved into me reading almost every book in her modest library, curled up on the bed in the front-porch bedroom of her home. Grandma Dahl was never without a book: You never knew when you might have a spare moment to read! She even brought them to the movie theater to get in a few moments of reading before the film started. I am just as obsessed with reading as Grandma was, and now I have a son who will burn the midnight oil to finish a good book. The legacy lives on!

Whether it is a special connection with your favorite teacher, a parent or even a geographical place, taking time to save those memories in your artwork preserves your lifelines to the past.

One of my favorite projects Carol created for this chapter is titled *My Babushka.* This artwork pays tribute to her cherished maternal grandmother, and I love that it captures the essence of Babushka's personality. The tactile quality of the beautiful domed box covered with elegant trims and weathered papers gives me a feeling for the style and appreciation of beauty that she had. It is a wonderful added bonus that more of Babushka's treasures and mementos can be stored inside.

One of my own favorite projects featured in this chapter is *Memories of Hartland,* which was inspired by stories my Grandma Dahl told to me as a little girl: tales of growing up in Hartland, Michigan. In this overflowing display of photos, I love looking at all the faces that shaped her world. I knew I had hit "memory pay dirt" when, as soon as my mother saw this piece of art, she asked if she could have it for her home!

We hope these projects commemorating our family histories will inspire you to forge some connections between your own family's past and today.

GRANDMA'S PURSE | by Carol

My grandmother was very conservative and modest in how she dressed, and her purses reflected

that severe style. The winter purse was black. The summer purse was ivory. The bags were

also large enough to hold all the things women carry with them. This fanciful little purse is

a **tongue-in-cheek tribute to my grandmother.** She loved color, and

she used vibrant fabrics to make quilts and accent pillows for her home. I think if Grandma

had lived in a different era, she would have loved a purse like this.

Begin to weave ribbons

Beginning at the top of the purse, on the inside so the ribbon's end is camouflaged, weave the ribbon in and out of the first "row" of wire.

Continue weaving ribbons

Continue weaving ribbons, changing the ribbon widths, patterns and textures frequently. Add a bit of fiber every few rows. Add ribbon to the purse handle, and tie several bows to the top corners.

Alter tag and add journaling

Alter a luggage tag to complement the purse. Create a mini accordion with journaling to fit inside the tag.

SUPPLIES
for the Technique

WIRE PURSE FORM *(Stampington)* OR OTHER WIRE FORM OF YOUR CHOICE

RIBBON *(May Arts, Making Memories)*

FIBERS *(optional)*

LUGGAGE TAG OR OTHER EMBELLISHMENT OF YOUR CHOICE

STRIP OF PAPER FOR JOURNALING

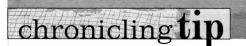

chronicling tip

AN ALTERNATIVE TO JOURNALING YOUR TRIBUTE IS PROVIDING KEY DESCRIPTIVE WORDS ABOUT THE PERSON YOUR PROJECT CHRONICLES. STAMP WORDS ONTO FLAT SHELL BUTTONS, PRINT THEM ONTO ADHESIVE TRANSPARENCIES AND ADHERE THEM TO CLEAR BUTTONS AND EXTRA-LARGE BRADS, OR STAMP THEM ONTO METAL-RIMMED ROUND TAGS. YOU MIGHT ALSO PRINT OUT TINY PHOTOS AND TRANSFER THE IMAGES ONTO THE SURFACES OF YOUR CHOICE. SIMPLY HAND-SEW OR WIRE YOUR VARIOUS EMBELLISHMENTS TO THE PURSE FORM.

A.R. DAHL | by Tena

❊ TECHNIQUE ❊ *Creating a spray-paint resist with ephemera*

While I was growing up, one of the **constants in my life** was my Grandpa Dahl. He came over every Sunday morning in his locksmith truck to visit with our family, and one of the children would get to ride home with him and spend the day at his house. I loved it when it was my turn. The inside of the locksmith truck was filled with tools and keys and boxes of stuff. I always thought my grandpa was a very important man to need so many important things. I love all the photos we have of him in his early years in the locksmith business. I especially loved that I was able to use some of the very keys from his business on my scrapbook layout to create this key-and-chain resist.

Spray paint over ephemera

Before spraying, cover your work area with newspaper. Position the items you are using to create the resist onto your background ledger paper. Spray paint lightly per the manufacturer's instructions. I wanted the ledger paper background to remain visible, so I used a very light coating of paint. Be sure to paint in a well-ventilated area or outdoors.

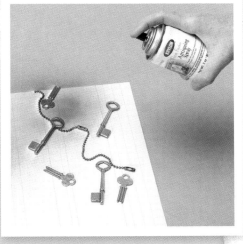

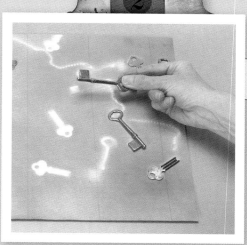

Lift up ephemera items to reveal resist

Wait a few minutes, then gently lift the ephemera off the painted background to reveal the resisted area.

Build page

Build your scrapbook page on top of the patterned paper you created. You may even incorporate the actual ephemera items if you wish. I also used an old stamp that my grandpa had used for his business in my layout.

SUPPLIES
for the Technique

EPHEMERA

LEDGER PAPER (*Making Memories*)

ANTIQUING SPRAY PAINT (*Krylon*)

NEWSPAPER

SUPPLIES
to Complete the Project

PHOTOS

PATTERNED CARDSTOCK
(*Three Bugs in a Rug*)

FABRIC (*Michael Miller*)

STAPLES (*Making Memories*)

ANTIQUE STAMP

ALPHABET STAMPS (*Cavalinni*)

INKS (*Ranger*)

ADHESIVE TRANSPARENCY (*Graphix*)

MONOADHESIVE (*Tombow USA*)

E-6000 GLUE

chronicling tip

CONSIDER USING OTHER TYPES OF EPHEMERA AND/OR TEXTURAL ITEMS, SUCH AS PAPER DOILIES OR LACE, TO CREATE A RESIST WITH THIS TECHNIQUE. YOU MIGHT ALSO TRY USING OTHER ART MEDIUMS, LIKE INK OR DIFFERENT PAINTS, TO APPLY COLOR.

tip TO AVOID STAINING YOUR EPHEMERA ITEMS, REMOVE THEM FROM THE PAPER WHILE THEY ARE STILL DAMP. QUICKLY WIPE THEM WITH A BABY WIPE AND RINSE THEM WITH WATER TO PREVENT THE PAINT FROM DISCOLORING THEM.

grandpa

❧ TECHNIQUE ❧ *Altering paper with Castaway ink and rubber stamps*

This project began with a coffee spill on my countertop. I cleaned the mess with a paper towel, and several hours later it dried into the shape of a dress, very much like what my mom wore in the 1950s. This "accidental art" became the central element in this layout about my mom and her sense of style. An accomplished seamstress, Mom has created beautifully tailored garments for herself and others throughout the years. This elegant paper towel dress is **the perfect tribute to my mother.**

Stamp Castaway onto cardstock

If your cardstock is coated, sand it lightly so the paper will accept the Castaway ink. Apply the Castaway ink to the stamp of your choice and apply the stamp to the cardstock to create a pattern. Allow the Castaway ink to penetrate the paper for about five minutes. While you wait, preheat a dry iron to the cotton setting.

Iron stamped paper

Iron over the entire paper. You'll see a change in color almost instantly.

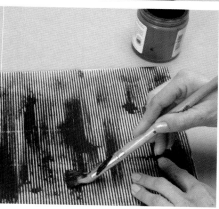

Paint corrugated paper with black gesso

Use a bristle brush to paint a piece of corrugated cardboard with black gesso, applying the paint heavily to some areas and lightly to others.

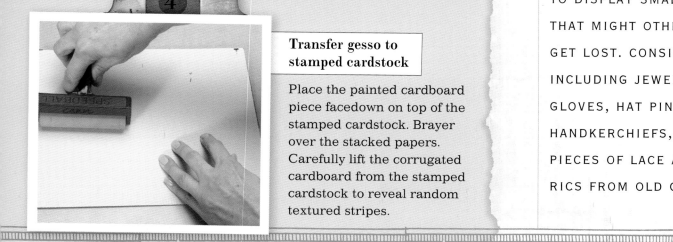

Transfer gesso to stamped cardstock

Place the painted cardboard piece facedown on top of the stamped cardstock. Brayer over the stacked papers. Carefully lift the corrugated cardboard from the stamped cardstock to reveal random textured stripes.

SUPPLIES
for the Technique

SOLID-COLORED UNCOATED CARDSTOCK

CASTAWAY *(Jacquard Products)*

RUBBER STAMPS *(100 Proof Press, Stampendous)*

IRON

BRISTLE BRUSH

CORRUGATED CARDBOARD

BLACK GESSO *(Golden)*

BRAYER

SUPPLIES
to Complete the Project

PRINTABLE COTTON *(Jacquard Products)*

JEWELS *(Heidi Swapp)* OR CHARMS

BELT BUCKLE *(7gypsies)*

PAPER FLOWER *(Doodlebug Design)*

BLACK VELVET RIBBON

MINI BLACK BUTTONS

SEWING MACHINE AND THREAD

UHU GLUE STICK

chronicling tip

ADDING DIMENSIONAL OBJECTS TO LAYOUTS ADDS INTEREST AND OFTEN HELPS TO DISPLAY SMALL ITEMS THAT MIGHT OTHERWISE GET LOST. CONSIDER INCLUDING JEWELRY, GLOVES, HAT PINS, HANDKERCHIEFS, BITS AND PIECES OF LACE AND FABRICS FROM OLD GARMENTS.

mom

❧ TECHNIQUE ❧ *Working with melted wax*

As a little girl, I spent a lot of time around my maternal grandmother, Babushka. She was a creative, hardworking woman who produced amazing handmade items with scraps of fabric and yarn. Babushka was a good teacher, patient and kind, and she allowed me to play with her collections of lace, fibers and buttons. She also provided old pots and pans for me to make "rose soup" out of spent rose blossoms. I miss Babushka greatly, and this little box is a tribute to her and the **sweet memories I have of our time together**.

Melt wax and brush onto project

Melt beeswax on the stove in an old double-boiler, in a mini crockpot for heating potpourri or in a specially designed product such as Ranger's "The Melting Pot." Make sure the wax does not get too hot (to prevent it from igniting). Protect your work area with newspaper or another covering. When the wax is fully melted, use a natural-hair bristle brush to apply the hot wax to your project. Work in small areas so you can apply the wax before it hardens.

Stamp into wax

Press a rubber stamp into the wax while it is still hot. Leave the stamp there and allow the wax to cool and set up for a minute. The rubber stamp releases quickly when the wax is sufficiently cool.

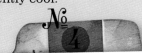

Apply metallic rub-ons to accent stamped areas

Use a makeup sponge to apply metallic rub-ons over the stamped wax to highlight the design. Lightly buff the wax in order to remove any excess rub-on.

Glue on muslin strips

Tear tea-dyed muslin into small rectangles. Glue the fabric onto a piece of chipboard cut to fit into the box. Glue the waxed panel onto the muslin strips. Journal the story on the back of the chipboard.

SUPPLIES
for the Technique

BEESWAX

POT TO MELT WAX

NEWSPAPER

NATURAL-HAIR BRISTLE BRUSH

RUBBER STAMP *(Stampendous)*

MAKEUP SPONGE

METALLIC RUB-ONS *(Craf-T Products)*

TEA-DYED MUSLIN

UHU GLUE STICK

CHIPBOARD

SUPPLIES
to Complete the Project

DOMED LID MEMORY BOX *(DCC)*

PAPER *(Autumn Leaves, 7gypsies, Creative Imaginations)*

COLLAGE IMAGES

METAL FRAME *(Pressed Petals)*

MONOGRAM COASTER *(Chronicle Books)*

MINI DOILY *(SEI)*

RUB-ONS *(Delish Designs, 7gypsies)*

BUTTONS

EYELET

RIBBON AND TRIM

LARGE SNAP *(Dritz)*

STAMPS *(Postmodern Design, Limited Edition)*

INK *(StazOn by Tsukineko, Ranger)*

grandmother

MEMORIES OF HARTLAND | by Tena

❧ TECHNIQUE ❧ *Constructing a framed collage*

I have albums and boxes of photos from my grandmother's youth and young adulthood in Hartland, Michigan. Grandma Dahl always shared the stories of her youth with me as I was growing up. As a young woman, she lived and worked in the Hartland boarding house run by her grandmother. I have always loved her photos of the people who shaped her world because **when I look at them, I see pieces of me.** I was named for my grandmother's mother, Tena Carter, who appears in many of the photos. I love that a framed collage of this size allows you to enjoy so many images in one place.

chronicling **tip**

MANY OF THE PHOTOS I SCANNED AND COPIED FOR THIS PROJECT HAD NOTES WRITTEN IN MY GRANDMOTHER'S AND GREAT-GRANDMOTHER'S HANDWRITING ON THE BACK. I SCANNED THE NOTES, COPIED THEM ONTO LEDGER PAPER AND USED THEM AS JOURNALING ON THE PROJECT. LITTLE ADDITIONS LIKE THESE HELP YOUR LOVED ONES' PERSONALITIES SHINE THROUGH.

SUPPLIES
for the Technique

PHOTOS FOR COLLAGE

LARGE FRAME *(North American Enclosures, Inc.)*

HEAVY CARDBOARD

FABRIC

CORK BACKING

CLEAR PACKING TAPE

BRAYER

RULER

STAPLER AND STAPLES

RUB 'N BUFF OIL PASTE *(AMACO)*

PENCIL

TACKY GLUE

STAPLE GUN AND STAPLES

SUPPLIES
to Complete the Project

PATTERNED PAPER *(Making Memories)*

RIBBON *(7gypsies)*

STICK PINS *(Making Memories, Dritz)*

grandmother

Lay out materials

Before you begin, lay out all the materials you'll need for the project: one large frame; two pieces of heavy cardboard cut to approximately 3" to 4" (8cm to 10cm) bigger than the frame; fabric approximately 5" (13cm) larger than the cardboard; cork to fit inside of the frame; clear packing tape; tacky glue; brayer; ruler; stapler. Apply some red and black Rub 'n Buff to the frame, if desired, to distress it.

Measure for cork placement

Place the frame on top of the layered cardboard pieces and mark the inside and outside corners.

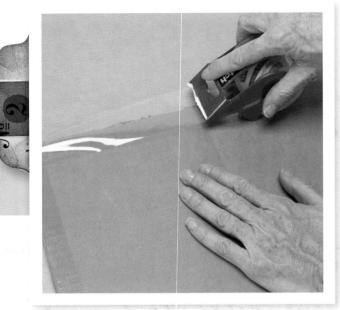

Adhere cardboard pieces together

Glue the two cardboard pieces together with tacky glue, then use clear packing tape to secure the edges.

Mark cork placement

Remove the frame and lay the cork (cut to the size of the inside of the frame) onto the cardboard with each corner touching the spots marked for the inside corners of the frame. Trace around the cork with a pencil to mark the exact placement.

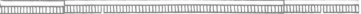

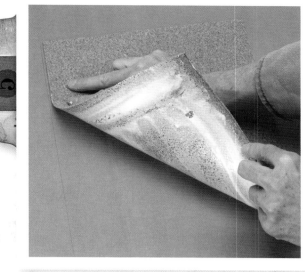

Adhere cork to cardboard

Apply tacky glue to one side of the cork piece and adhere it to the cardboard inside the lines you drew.

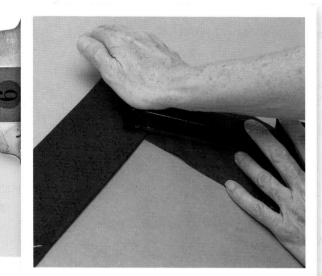

Secure fabric to cardboard and cork sandwich

Lay the fabric over the layered cardboard and cork, then flip the sandwich over. Pull the fabric taut to cover the cardboard, and secure it at the back with staples.

Secure pictures and frame

Arrange the photos as you like, then staple them in place, using the frame as a guide to see which photos fall inside the frame and which photos peek out beyond its edge. Secure the frame on top of the collage by using a heavyweight staple gun and stapling the frame to the mat from the back side of the photo mat.

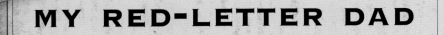

MY RED-LETTER DAD | by Carol

My dad and I **share** the kind of **special relationship** that can only be enjoyed by a father and a daughter—and this makes it easy for me to create memorable pieces of art from his photos. I especially enjoy snapshots of his younger years; they have a "movie star" quality about them. When I was contemplating the theme for this project, I thought of the phrase "red-letter day." I knew that "red-letter" indicated something good, but I didn't know its origins. I did some research and found out that the term was originally used to mark a holy day in a church calendar. It later became a way to designate days of special significance. What an appropriate phrase to describe my dad, a special person in my life on all days.

chronicling **tip**

USE SPECIAL WORDS OR PHRASES WITH HISTORICAL BACKGROUND TO INSPIRE A TITLE OR THEME. ONCE A THEME IS ESTABLISHED, IT IS MUCH EASIER TO KEEP YOUR THOUGHTS COLLECTED AND ORGANIZED.

SUPPLIES
for the Technique

PHOTO

TONER-BASED PHOTOCOPIER

PLAIN WHITE PAPER

SCISSORS

OIL PAINT AND GUM ARABIC *(Winsor & Newton)*

SPONGE

PALETTE PAPER *(Loew-Cornell)*

LINSEED OIL *(Grumbacher)*

BRAYER

SPRAY BOTTLE WITH WATER

HOT-PRESS WATERCOLOR PAPER *(Strathmore)* OR OTHER PROJECT SURFACE ON WHICH TO TRANSFER IMAGE

SPOON

SUPPLIES
to Complete the Project

PATTERNED PAPER *(7gypsies)*

INDEX CARD ALPHABET GUIDES *(Esselte)*

TWILL LETTER TABS *(Carolee's Creations)*

ALPHABET FABRIC

TAGS *(Avery Dennison)*

STAMPS *(EK Success, Limited Edition, Stampington)*

INK-JET TRANSPARENCY *(3M)*

JOURNALING SPOTS *(Heidi Swapp)*

FILE FOLDER CLIPS *(Junkitz)*

RED TWILL

INK *(Ranger)*

HOLE PUNCH

UHU GLUE STICK

TACKY GLUE

dad

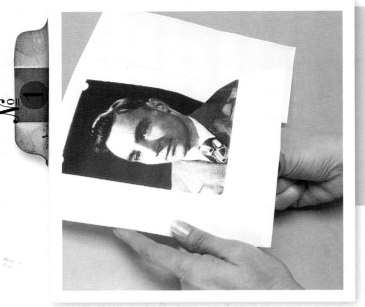

Make copies of photo and cut out

Make several toner-based copies of the photo you wish to transfer (ink-jet copies will not work) on plain white paper. If there are numbers or letters on the original photo, you will need to reverse the image on the copy. Cut out the photocopied image so that only the image you want to transfer remains. (In this example I cut away everything but the silhouette of the head and the shoulders.)

Apply gum arabic to photocopied image

Apply gum arabic to the copy, rubbing it in gently with your fingers on both the back and front sides of the copy. It's important to saturate the entire copy with gum arabic, but don't allow it to pool on the surface of the copy. Continue to rub in the gum arabic until the surface feels dry and no longer tacky.

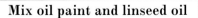

Rub away any excess gum arabic with a damp sponge

Use a damp sponge to gently rub away any excess gum arabic remaining on the surface of the photocopied image.

Mix oil paint and linseed oil

Squeeze a small amount of oil paint onto palette paper or a piece of glass. Add a drop or two of linseed oil to make the paint smooth. Roll over the mixture with a brayer until the paint is smooth and flat on the surface.

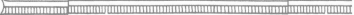

No 5

Brayer paint mixture onto photocopied image

Use the brayer to apply the paint mixture to the photocopied image. Apply the paint in a layer that covers the image but that is not too thick. The image should remain visible behind the paint.

No 6

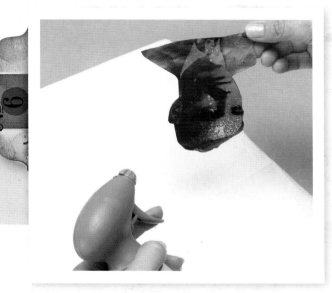

Dampen the painted surface of the image

Use a spray bottle to dampen the painted surface of the image with water. The paint should start rolling off the light-colored areas of the photocopy. Continue to spray the image with water until all the excess paint is removed.

No 7

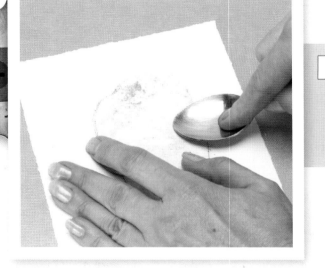

Lift up photocopy to reveal image transfer

Carefully lift up the photocopy and the palette paper to reveal the transferred image. You may repeat this process onto another surface. In fact, the image used on the cover of this book is a second-generation print.

No 8

Transfer image onto receiving surface

Select the surface onto which you'll transfer your image. I used smooth, durable hot-press watercolor paper. Gently place the photocopy, image-side-down, onto the watercolor paper. Place a piece of palette paper on top of the photocopy. Use a spoon to gently rub the back of the image, making sure that all areas are rubbed consistently.

GREAT-AUNT NET

by Tena

I think we all have **someone** in our family **who is larger than life**. My Great-Aunt Net was always that person for me, as well as for my mother when she was a little girl. Aunt Net always looked like a movie star to me. She wore beautiful clothes, her long blonde hair was always done up in a French twist and her nails were always perfectly manicured. When we went to visit her in Florida or she came to stay at our house it was a wonderful treat. We have lots of photos of Aunt Net in her younger years, when she owned a lingerie store in Hollywood and was married to a championship billiard player whom she traveled and even competed with. I created this display box, adorned with etched stampboard tiles, to commemorate her glamourous style.

SUPPLIES
for the Technique

STAMPBOARD TILES *(Ampersand)*

FOAM APPLICATOR

COLORED INKS *(Ranger, Stampin' Up, Superior)*

CLEAR EMBOSSING INK

RUBBER STAMPS *(Sunday International)*

EMBOSSING POWDER *(Ranger)*

HEAT GUN

STAMPBOARD SCRATCH TOOL *(Ampersand)*

DISTRESSING TOOL

SUPPLIES
to Complete the Project

CIGAR BOX

PATTERNED PAPER *(Captured Elements, Fancy Pants)*

PARCHMENT PAPER AND ENVELOPE

FOAM ADHESIVE SHEET *(7gypsies)*

METAL PHOTO CORNERS *(K&Company)*

RIBBON *(7gypsies)*

METAL CLIP *(7gypsies)*

JUMP RING *(Making Memories)*

BRAYER

GLUE STICK

E-6000 GLUE

chronicling **tip**

USE A PIECE OF STATIONERY AND AN OFFICE SUPPLY ENVELOPE TO HOUSE THE JOURNALING FOR YOUR PROJECT. OR, WRITE YOUR JOURNALING IN THE STYLE OF A PERSONAL LETTER DESCRIBING THE EVENTS OR THE PERSON YOU ARE MEMORIALIZING IN YOUR ARTWORK.

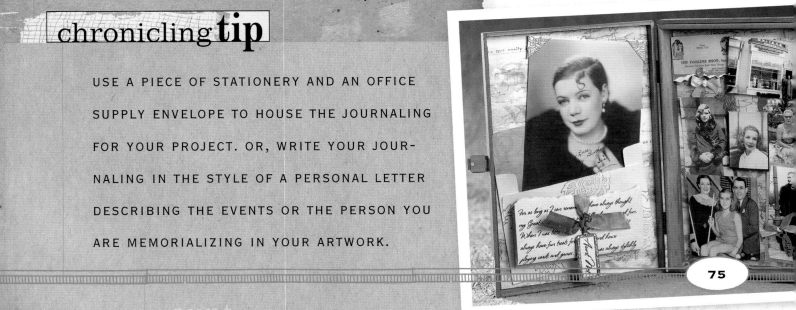

aunt

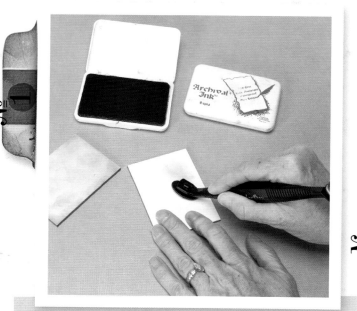

Apply ink to stampboard tiles

Use a foam applicator to apply different colored inks to the stampboard tiles.

Stamp tiles with clear embossing ink

Apply clear embossing ink to a stamp of your choice and stamp each stampboard tile with the clear ink.

Sprinkle embossing powder onto stamped tiles

Sprinkle the stamped area with embossing powder, covering the clear ink completely. Tap the tile lightly against your work surface so the extra powder falls away.

Heat-set embossing powder

Use a heat gun to set the embossing powder, creating raised lines.

№ 5

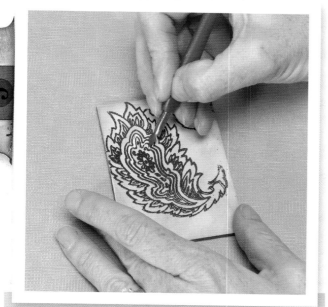

Scratch away colored ink

Use a pointed stampboard tool to scratch away color in different areas of the stamped design.

№ 6

Sand edges of stampboard tiles

Use a distressing tool to sand some color from the edges of the stampboard tiles.

construction **notes**

To assemble your tribute box, use a brayer and a glue stick to adhere patterned paper to the front and inside of a cigar box. Use E-6000 glue to adhere tiles to the front of the box in the desired pattern, and allow it to dry overnight. Adhere the photos and journaling inside the cigar box using the adhesive of your choice.

she gave me
wings to fly

STEPHANIE MCATEE

This canvas is very personal to me. It's the first piece of artwork I've done on my mom, whom I unexpectedly lost sixteen years ago when she was only forty-two. We all go through processes in life, and we all evolve in our own timing. It took me this long to be able to focus on my mom in my art. I wanted to make a visual tribute that I could hang in my home and see

every day. I used her favorite color, red, and a simplistic design that leaves the focus on her photos. The message, my handwriting impressed into beeswax, tells the story of how she recognized my art before I did. She strongly encouraged me to pursue art; she gave me the wings to fly.

women
who create

KATHERINE BROOKS

I absolutely love how this layout came together. I come from a long line of women who have been amazing artists, each in her own way, and I wanted to honor them. By teaching me to knit, sew, cook and even make porcelain, each has touched my life in one way or another. I tried to incorporate items from the past, such as the old lace from Germany that my mother used on one of my dresses as a child.

barb**ara**
CÉLINE NAVARRO

I miss my sister. She died several months ago at the age of twenty. Most of my art pieces are dedicated to her, and this piece is no exception. I wanted to celebrate her love for life with colorful fabric, paints and beautiful photographs I took of her. All I can do now is celebrate her memory the best way I can and hope that she enjoys this fabric art tribute journal.

tena**carter**
TENA SPRENGER

I ndependent woman, my Great Grandmother, my namesake

Whenever I tell people how to spell my name, I say, "Tena with an 'e'," and they usually reply, "My, that's an interesting spelling." I was named after my maternal great-grandmother, Tena Carter, who was a strong and industrious woman. When my grandmother was a little girl both she and my great-grandmother worked to earn their room, board and wages in the boarding house owned by my great-great-grandparents. It made for an interesting life! Tena was an independent, hardworking woman. I have always loved sharing her name.

sisters
TENA SPRENGER

My mom was part of a family of six children growing up, and many of my favorite pictures of her early years are those of my mom and her older sister, Diana. Diana and Darlene were the two oldest children in the family and only a couple years apart in age. They couldn't have looked more different: Diana had long ringlets of thick dark hair and Darlene had hardly any hair those first couple years. The friendship they forged as children remained strong in their adult years, and Diana's daughter Dana is like a sister to me today.

the way I see
my life
CAROL WINGERT

I am amazed how often I will do or say
something and then think, "My mom
says that!" or, "Grandpa used to do
that!" I wanted to preserve the fact
that my family members contributed
to how I see life. I altered an eyeglass
case with papers, fabric and ribbon,
then cut out headshots of my
parents and grandparents.
I finished by inserting a quote
behind an old pair of eyeglasses
that I had found in a parking lot.

a special
touch
CAROL WINGERT

My father-in-law related a story
to me about this stray horse
that appeared on his family's
farm. He stayed with the horse
to keep it calm while one of his
brothers ran to the barn to get
a halter and lead rope. Dad
appears to have had a special
touch with this horse. I think he
has a soft spot for animals, even
though he doesn't say much
about them. This collage was
assembled on an old book jack-
et, which was then glued onto a
piece of walnut ink-sprayed mat
board. I stamped the flourishes
and then inserted the piece into
an old frame, which I sanded
and painted black.

ME(tena)

It's GOOD TO BE(

Express Yourself
by Carol

Have you ever thought about your ancestors and wondered what they were really like? What did they do with their time? What were some of their routines? What chores did they like? Which ones did they dislike? What were their favorite colors? What were their dreams and goals? Generations down the road, your great-great-grandchildren might be looking at pictures of you and wondering the same things. This was part of my inspiration for embarking on the new adventure of expressing myself through personal journals and memory art. I didn't want future generations wondering what I was like as a person. I wanted them to be able to read and see for themselves. Expressing yourself doesn't have to be deep, it doesn't have to reveal all of your innermost personal thoughts, and—guess what?—it doesn't have to be filled with angst. Sharing your favorite foods, vacation highlights, things you believe in and value most—these are things that are comfortable for you to write about and interesting for others to read.

One of Tena's projects that I totally enjoyed was her *Artful Excursion*. I love how she showed pictures of her workspace in reality, not cleaned up for a glamour shot. It made me smile when I read her journaling about how much she loves her job and how she gets to wake up each day and create art to earn her living. Her contemporary presentation of photos and journaling in a layered, dimensional format was both artistic and personal. I think her wall art is a wonderful piece of self-expression.

My favorite among the projects I created for this chapter is my personal art journal titled *Coffee Spoons*. It is based on a T.S. Eliot quote about living life day-to-day, and it contains snippets of my daily life, from the mundane to my goals and dreams. Once I started creating the journal, I didn't want to stop making additional pages. I even clipped in some things for use in the future; I have all sorts of ideas for more pages. See what a monster this self-expression inspiration has unleashed?

I challenge you to make yourself a promise: You will take the time to focus some of your creativity on yourself. Ask your family to take pictures of you, or take silly self-portraits to stir your creative imagination. Explore your different moods, your feelings, your likes and dislikes, and your connections to others. Document your personal tapestry—that weaving that is individually and uniquely yours. Tell your story!

DON'T BLINK | by Tena

DON'T

BLINK

LIFE   MOVES   FAST

When most of us start scrapbooking, we have a tendency to chronicle events and occasions. But I've found that some of my favorite scrapbooking layouts and photo art projects feature **photos of everyday activities** and ordinary moments. So I made a commitment to myself to try to take pictures of something every single day in hopes of creating a better time capsule of what our life is truly like. This little book is titled Blink because some of these photos almost didn't get taken. I just happened to have a camera on me, and I ended up with some of my favorite shots of the year. I didn't add any journaling, because the story is told by the expressions and emotions on the faces of the people I love. These faux glazed tiles give the project a vibrant cover.

SUPPLIES
for the Technique

CARDSTOCK

1¼" (3CM) SQUARE PUNCH

¾" (2CM) SQUARE PUNCH

GLAZE PEN *(Sakura)*

DIAMOND GLAZE *(JudiKins)*

PALETTE DISH

INEXPENSIVE PAINTBRUSH

WAX PAPER

RUB-ONS *(Veer, KI Memories, Scenic Route, 7gypsies)*

SUPPLIES
to Complete the Project

CHIPBOARD SPIRAL BOOK *(7gypsies)*

CHIPBOARD LETTERS *(Magistical Memories)*

ACRYLIC PAINT *(DecoArt)*

RIBBON *(May Arts, Midori, Offray, American Crafts)*

ADHESIVE

chronicling **tip**

PAINT DIAMOND GLAZE ONTO PATTERNED PAPER TO CHANGE ITS APPEARANCE AND STIFFEN THE PAPER. WHEN POURED INTO A MOLD, DIAMOND GLAZE CAN CREATE THE ILLUSION OF A GLASSLIKE SURFACE.

every day

Punch out cardstock squares

Use both sizes of square punches to punch out cardstock squares.

Outline edges of square tiles

Use a glaze pen to draw in a rough outline around the edges of each tile.

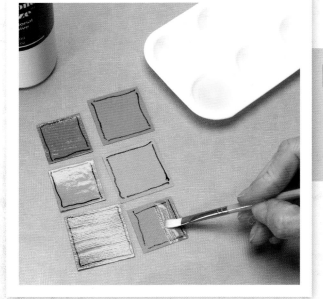

Paint Diamond Glaze onto tiles

Pour some Diamond Glaze into a palette dish and use an inexpensive paintbrush to apply the glaze to the cardstock tiles. Allow the tiles to dry on wax paper to avoid their sticking to your work surface.

tip DIAMOND GLAZE IS ALSO FUN TO USE TO FILL IN FRAMES OR RECESSED AREAS ON YOUR ARTWORK TO CREATE FAUX GLASS EFFECTS OR STAINED GLASS EFFECTS.

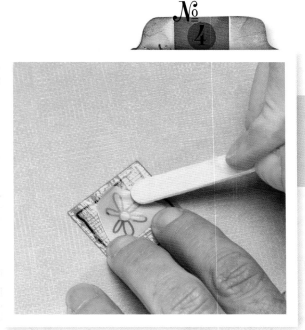

Add accents to tiles

Apply rub-ons to the tiles or add text or images to them with a glaze pen.

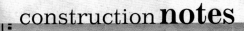

construction **notes**

To make a book like this, begin with a premade chipboard book. First paint the book with acrylic paint, then mount your faux glazed tiles on the cover. The title letters shown here are made of chipboard; they were first painted with acrylic paint and then coated with Diamond Glaze to give them a shiny finish before adhering them to the cover of the book. The additional words in the cover title were added using rub-on letters. To embellish the spine, pieces of ribbon were tied onto the coils.

COFFEE SPOONS | by Carol

i have measured out my life with coffee spoons.

-T. S. ELIOT-

When I first read this quote from T.S. Eliot, I wasn't thinking about its meaning, just that it would make a great title for my personal journal—especially paired with vintage tea/coffee spoons, altered with rub-ons for an extra unique touch. After I formatted the journal in my head, though, I began thinking more about the meaning of the words. I think T.S. Eliot was saying that **life is to be taken day-by-day**, in small measure, so the benefits of each day are not missed. Too much focus on the future can cause us to lose our enjoyment of the present.

SUPPLIES
for the Technique

SPOONS

RUB-ONS *(Dee's Designs, My Mind's Eye)*

POPSICLE STICK

MATTE SEALER *(Krylon)*

SUPPLIES
to Complete the Project

CHIPBOARD SPIRAL BOOK *(7gypsies)*

CHIPBOARD LETTERS
(Magistical Memories)

ACRYLIC PAINT *(DecoArt)*

RIBBON *(May Arts, Midori, Offray, American Crafts)*

ADHESIVE

chronicling **tip**

CONSISTENTLY KEEPING A HANDWRITTEN JOURNAL HAS ALWAYS BEEN MORE OF A CHORE THAN A PLEASURE FOR ME. BY ADDING PHOTOS AND OTHER ARTWORK TO CREATE AN ART JOURNAL, I HAVE BEEN INSPIRED TO MORE CONSISTENTLY CHRONICLE PARTS OF MY LIFE.

self

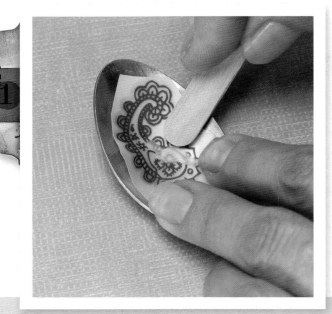

№ 1

Apply rub-on to spoon

Make sure the surface to which you'll adhere the rub-on is clean and dry. Follow the manufacturer's instructions to carefully rub the pattern onto the bowl of the spoon. Use your fingers to massage the rub-on into the rounded areas.

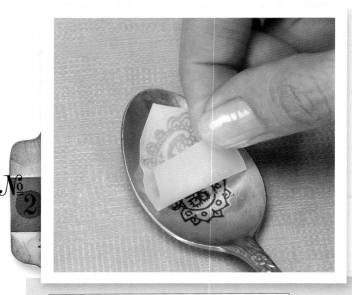

№ 2

Lift away rub-on carrier to reveal transferred image

Gently peel back the rub-on carrier to reveal the image now adhered to the spoon.

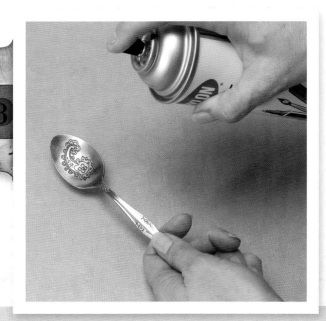

№ 3

Spray item with sealer

Spray matte sealer onto the item with the rub-on image to secure it.

Variations

This same process may be applied to a variety of household items, such as decorative glassware, candles, decorative plates, wooden plaques, wooden or ceramic trays, etc. (Just be aware that it's not advisable to eat off of or drink out of these items once they are altered this way.)

construction **notes**

Alter a ceramic plate or platter to commemorate a special day, such as a birthday or a wedding. Transfer a photographic image into the center of the plate or platter with a Lazertran method (as seen in our first book, *Artful Memories*), then use alphabet and number rub-ons to apply the names and date to the rim. Hang on a wall or display on a plate shelf.

SEW WONDERFUL | by Tena

Ever since I was a very small child, sewing has been a big part of my life. Some of my earliest memories are of sitting on the floor playing with my toys listening to **the hum of my mom's sewing machine.** By the time I was five years old, I had made my first hand-sewn creation, and I haven't stopped since. My *Sew Wonderful* book shares some of the highlights and inspirations from my sewing history. The weathered parchment paper enhances the feeling of nostalgia.

PARCHMENT PAPER OR TEXT-WEIGHT PAPER

IRON *(optional)*

INK PAD *(StazOn by Tsukineko)*

FOAM BRUSH

MOD PODGE *(Plaid)* OR ANOTHER DÉCOUPAGE MEDIUM

SCISSORS OR HOLE PUNCHES *(optional)*

SUPPLIES
to Complete the Project

PATTERNED CARDSTOCK *(7gypsies, Captured Elements, Autumn Leaves)*

SOLID-COLORED CARDSTOCK

FABRIC *(Alexander Fabrics)*

PINK JOURNALING SQUARE *(Heidi Swapp)*

ALPHABET STAMPS *(Postmodern Design, FontWerks)*

JOURNALING PEN *(Zig Millennium)*

RIBBONS AND TRIMS *(May Arts, Midori, Offray)*

BUTTONS *(7gypsies, SEI, Michael Levine)*

SMALL WOODEN SPOOLS

STAPLES *(Making Memories)*

HEART PUNCHES

THREAD *(Coats and Clark)*

EYELET LACE BORDER PUNCH *(Fiskars)*

CHALK *(Deluxe Designs)*

STICK PINS *(Heidi Grace)*

STANDARD HOLE PUNCH

SCREW POSTS

PINKING SHEARS *(Fiskars)*

MONOADHESIVE *(Tombow USA)*

TACKY GLUE

E-6000 GLUE

chronicling **tip**

SINCE THIS WAS A SEWING-THEMED BOOK, I EDGED MY PAGES WITH PINKING SHEARS AND ADDED SMALL STITCHED DETAILS WHENEVER POSSIBLE THROUGHOUT THE BOOK. CONSIDER CAREFULLY CHOOSING SMALL DETAILS LIKE PAGE EDGES, FONTS OR FABRICS TO TIE A THEMED BOOK TOGETHER.

family

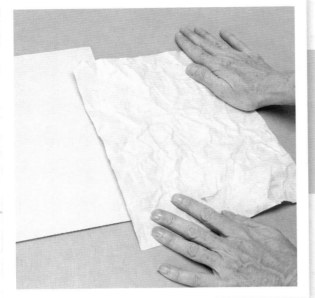

Crumple paper

Gently crumple parchment paper or text-weight paper into a ball, being careful not to tear the paper. Flatten out the crumpled paper with your hands. If you desire a flatter surface, use an iron on low heat.

Apply ink to wrinkles

Lightly brush an ink pad across the top of the creases and wrinkles in the paper to highlight the distressed areas.

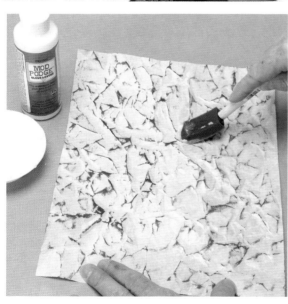

Apply découpage medium to paper

Using a foam brush, apply a light coat of Mod Podge or another découpage medium over the entire surface of the paper and allow it to dry.

tip DISTRESSING IS A GREAT WAY TO ADD TEXTURE WITHOUT ADDING BULK TO YOUR ARTWORK. TRY USING IT ON MEDIUM BROWN TONE PAPER TO CREATE THE ILLUSION OF LEATHER.

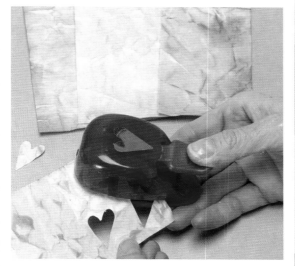

Use paper for pages or for accents

Use entire sheets of paper for book pages, or cut shapes from the paper to use as accents.

twin sundresse

ery Hot Pants

very groovy peasan

construction **notes**

The pages of this handmade book have been punched with three holes using a standard hole punch and bound together using three medium-sized screw posts. A much thicker book could be created using a longer screw post.

I had watched Mom sew and now the needle & thread was in my hands. Armed with fabric scraps and old pantyhose for stuffing I set about creating my doll. She is cherished to this day.

THINGS I VALUE MOST | by Carol

❧ TECHNIQUE ❧ *Stamping into partially hardened modeling paste*

I wanted to create a project that expresses the things I value most in a succinct and easy-to-read format. **I believe what we value affects our behaviors and our decisions.** Values, in my opinion, create the basis for character. I love the way stamping these meaningful words into modeling paste really gave them dimension.

№ 1

Apply modeling paste to framing mat

Use a spatula or palette knife to apply lightweight modeling paste to the surface of a framing mat. Paste may be applied with heavy texture or worked to a smooth finish, depending upon preference.

SUPPLIES
for the Technique

FRAMING MAT

PALETTE KNIFE OR SPATULA

LIGHTWEIGHT MODELING PASTE *(Liquitex)*

RUBBER STAMPS *(The Missing Link Stamp Co., Limited Edition, Postmodern Design, FontWerx, Stampotique)*

BLACK INK *(Clearsnap, Inc.)*

CHALK INK *(Clearsnap, Inc.)*

GLAZE *(Golden)*

ACRYLIC PAINT *(Jacquard) (optional)*

PAINTBRUSH *(optional)*

№ 2

Stamp into paste with black ink

Allow the paste to dry almost completely, then press inked stamps directly into the surface of the paste. Be careful not to rock the stamped image, as that distorts the letters. Slowly release the rubber stamp from the paste and immediately clean away any paste stuck to the rubber. Repeat with other inked rubber stamps. Allow the frame to dry completely.

SUPPLIES
to Complete the Project

GESSO *(Golden)*

PAPER *(Bo-Bunny Press)*

BRADS *(SEI)*

PVA GLUE

chronicling**tip**

HERE I CHOSE APPROPRIATE WORDS TO FRAME THIS PHOTO, BUT YOU MIGHT ALSO USE A FAVORITE QUOTE OR RELEVANT NAMES AND DATES, SUCH AS A WEDDING DAY OR DATE OF BIRTH. YOU MAY ALSO WANT TO ADD A SMALL WOODEN FRAME AROUND THE STAMPED MAT.

№ 3

Apply chalk ink and paint to frame

Apply chalk ink directly to the frame to add color. Allow the ink to dry completely. Because the chalk ink color was not the exact tone I needed, I also applied acrylic paint to the frame surface using a dry paintbrush. Allow paint to dry completely. Coat the frame with a clear or white glaze to seal.

me

BITS AND PIECES OF THE CREATIVE ME

by Carol

✻ TECHNIQUE ✻ *Creating a faux stained glass effect*

Over the past few years, I have noticed certain patterns emerging in my work and in **my creative habits.** I decided to take a few of these patterns and incorporate them into a funky mini book. Here are a few of the "bits" I included:

* My muse is an early bird.

* I adore paisley, dress forms and torsos.

* I seriously love numbers, letters and fonts.

* Fabrics and buttons are basic to my creativity.

* Nature is one of my greatest sources of inspiration.

The faux broken glass/stained glass effect I created for this project enhanced my theme.

SUPPLIES
for the Technique

CARDSTOCK OR OTHER HEAVYWEIGHT PAPER

ACRYLIC PAINT *(Making Memories)*

MEDIUM-SIZED PAINTBRUSH

SMALL DETAIL PAINTBRUSH

LOW-TACK MASKING TAPE *(3M)*

SUPPLIES
to Complete the Project

MINI BOOK *(Pixie Press)*

CHIPBOARD AND MASK LETTERS *(Heidi Swapp)*

RUBBER STAMPS *(Hero Arts, EK Success, Inkadinkado, PSX, Paper Inspirations, Limited Edition, Sandi Miller, Stampers Anonymous, Anima Designs, Sunday International)*

INK *(Clearsnap)*

LABELS *(Dymo)*

RIBBON *(Midori)*

BUTTONS *(FoofaLa)*

GLAZE PEN *(Sakura)*

GESSO *(Golden)*

PVA GLUE

GLUE STICK

BRAYER

chronicling **tip**

THE PLAYFUL, ART JOURNAL-STYLE OF THIS BOOK IS REFLECTED IN THE CHOICE OF PAINT COLORS AND IN THE METHOD OF PRESENTATION. TO CREATE A MORE ELEGANT LOOK, USE A DARK BACKGROUND PAINT AND THEN PAINT OVER THE MASKING TAPE WITH COLORED OR STANDARD METALLIC PAINTS. THE PAINT COLOR CAN CHANGE THE LOOK OF THE BOOK ENTIRELY.

family

Paint background

Choose a paper that is at least the thickness of cardstock. Paint the paper or other surface you wish to alter with a dark color, or a color that will contrast strongly with the other colors on the page. The background paint will be visible as "cracks" or grout lines. Allow the paint to dry completely.

Tear low-tack masking tape into strips

Cut or tear low-tack masking tape into thin strips.

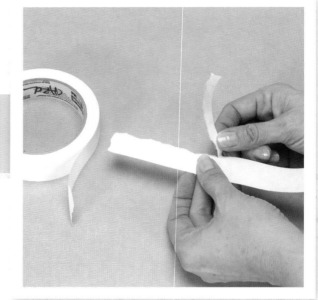

Adhere low-tack masking tape to painted surface

Place the tape onto the painted surface in whatever pattern you choose. Press over the tape with your fingers to make sure it is firmly in place.

tip FOR THE PAGE SHOWN IN THE STEP-BY-STEP INSTRUCTIONS, I CREATED A GRID PATTERN WITH MASKING TAPE. YOU MAY TRY OTHER PATTERNS, AS WELL: ADHERE THE TAPE IN RANDOM SECTIONS AND AT ANGLES TO CREATE A STAINED GLASS EFFECT, OR IN LINES FOR JOURNALING, OR IN SQUARES OR RECTANGLES FOR FRAMES. YOU DECIDE.

Apply paint over taped areas

Use a small paintbrush to brush one or multiple colors onto the taped areas. Be careful not to load up the paintbush too heavily, or the paint will seep under the masking tape. It's better to lightly paint over the surface several times than to ruin the clean lines by using too much paint. Allow the paint to dry thoroughly.

Peel off masking tape

Carefully peel off the masking tape to reveal the dark paint lines between the colored squares.

ARTFUL EXCURSION | by Tena

Every morning I get up and prepare for a new "Artful excursion". I am usually not going further than my home art space, but that's ok. Everything I need is right in front of me; my paints, inks, stamps, photos, books and laptop. Somedays I travel very far others I can't even get the creative engine started. So lucky am I to have art as my job and journey every day.

artful EXCURSION

love my job

ME (tena)

I love my job. Sometimes I can't believe it's true that I get to wake up every morning and create art to earn my living. I am one lucky girl. This collage is a tribute of sorts to the "Artful Excursion" I get to take every weekday morning when I go to work in the downstairs office in my house (also known as the messy art room). **Some days my creative mojo is really flowing,** and other days not so much, but I wouldn't trade this job for anything. This fun image transfer technique helped me to celebrate this aspect of my life in this expressive project.

SUPPLIES
for the Technique

HIGH-CONTRAST IMAGE

TONER-BASED PHOTOCOPIER

PLAIN TEXT-WEIGHT PAPER

IMAGE TRANSFER MATERIAL SHEET (*PaperWERX*)

SCISSORS

BONE FOLDER

TRAY OF WARM WATER

LINT-FREE TOWEL

GEL MEDIUM

SUPPLIES
to Complete the Project

FRAME WITH GLASS INSERT

PHOTO MAT

COLLAGE MATERIALS (PHOTOS, JOURNALING, ETC.)

CHIPBOARD

PATTERNED PAPER (*SEI, Making Memories, Rusty Pickle*)

ADHESIVE TRANSPARENCY (*Grafix*)

FABRIC FLOWERS (*Heidi Swapp*)

RUB-ONS (*7gypsies, Creative Imaginations, Autumn Leaves*)

FOAM STAMPS (*Making Memories*)

INKS (*StazOn by Tsukineko*)

ACRYLIC PAINTS (*Making Memories, Delta*)

BUTTONS (*SEI, FoofaLa*)

FABRIC APPLIQUE FLOURISH (*FoofaLa*)

PAPER PUNCHES (*EK Success*)

SMALL WOODEN SPOOLS

STAPLES (*Making Memories*)

JOURNALING PEN (*Zig Millennium*)

GLAZE PENS (*Sakura*)

MONOADHESIVE (*Tombow USA*)

E-6000

TACKY GLUE

chronicling **tip**

IMAGE TRANSFERS ONTO GLASS ARE A GREAT WAY TO ADD DIMENSION WITHOUT ADDING WEIGHT TO YOUR PROJECT. THESE SAME TYPES OF IMAGE TRANSFERS WORK WELL ON WOOD, METAL AND PLASTIC, TOO.

·me

Make toner-based copy of image

Make a toner-based copy (using a standard copy machine) of a high-contrast image onto plain copy paper.

Adhere image transfer material sheet to photocopy

Trim the photocopied image and the image transfer material sheet down to the same size. Remove the protective backing from the transfer sheet and adhere the transfer sheet to the right side of the photocopied image. Turn the fused sheets over so the blank side of the paper faces up. Use a bone folder to burnish over the photocopied image. Flip the fused sheets over so the image faces up and burnish again, being careful not to press too hard.

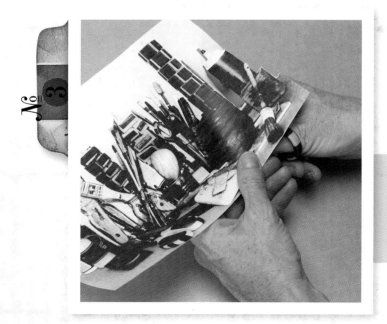

Cut out image

Use small scissors to carefully cut out the image you want to transfer.

Submerge image in warm water

Submerge the cut-out image in a tray of warm water and let it soak for 5–7 minutes.

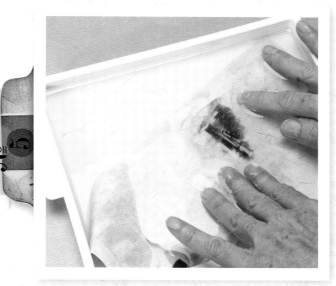

Rub away paper backing

When the image is fully saturated, gently rub away the paper backing. Be careful not to rub too hard so you don't rip the image transfer.

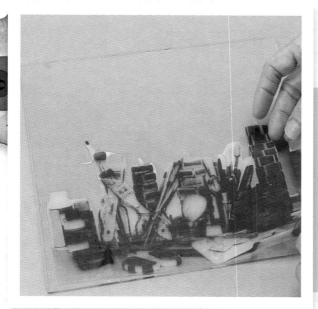

Adhere image transfer to your project surface

Remove the image transfer from the water and dry lightly with a lint-free towel. Let the transfer air dry for a while until it is completely dry. There is usually enough adhesive left on the back of the transfer to attach it to the project. If no stickiness remains, however, apply a small amount of gel medium to the back of the transfer to attach it to the surface of the project.

construction **notes**

Here I transferred the image onto the glass portion of the frame. Then I composed the balance of the collage and journaling on the photo mat, which I then inserted behind the glass inside the frame. You can add further dimension to your framed collage by gluing additional elements to the exterior of the frame.

The inspiration for this project came from something I used to say to Ashley: "Yes, you are the Princess, but I'm still the Queen." I used the line to signify that a subject was no longer open for discussion. This book is a bit of a parody. Those who know me would vouch that I'm down to earth and do not have a "queenly" attitude. As illustrated in my little piano-hinged book, my castle is just a house and my throne is a bent willow outdoor chair. Webster defines a queen as a woman who is the sovereign of a kingdom, the wife of a king, or pre-eminent or majestic. To me, **being a queen** is all about being a strong leader and mentor, being fair, approachable and confident, being a creative problem-solver and being respected by people I care about.

SUPPLIES
for the Technique

NINE PIECES OF CARDSTOCK

RULER

SCISSORS OR A PAPER CUTTER

TEMPLATE *(page 127)*

BONE FOLDER

PAPER CLIPS

PENCIL *(optional)*

SEVEN BAMBOO STICKS

ACRYLIC PAINT OR GESSO *(Golden)*

PVA GLUE

PAINTBRUSH

GARDEN SHEARS OR STRONG OLD SCISSORS

SUPPLIES
to Complete the Project

PAPER *(Three Bugs in a Rug)*

CHIPBOARD LETTERS *(Heidi Swapp, Pressed Petals)*

EMBROIDERED LETTERS *(EK Success)*

FILM NEGATIVE STRIPS

RUB-ONS *(My Mind's Eye, 7gypsies)*

METALLIC SCRAP CROWNS

RUBBER STAMPS *(Hero Arts, Stampers Anonymous, Limited Edition)*

INK *(Clearsnap)*

RIBBON *(May Art)*

CHARMS *(Flair Designs, 7gypsies, Anima Designs)*

GLUE STICK

ADHESIVE TABS *(Hermafix)*

chronicling **tip**

A STRIP OF PHOTOS IS A GREAT WAY TO DISPLAY MANY IMAGES IN A SMALL AREA. FIRST, SCAN AND SIZE PHOTOS TO FIT A FILM NEGATIVE STRIP AND TEMPORARILY ADHERE THE PHOTOS TO THE NEGATIVE. THEN, MAKE A BLACK-AND-WHITE PHOTOCOPY OF THE STRIP ONTO WHITE CARDSTOCK.

family

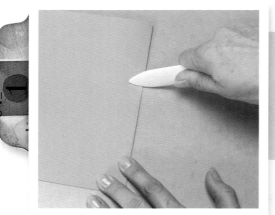

Fold paper in half to make pages

Cut 8 pieces of cardstock to 7¾" x 11" (20cm x 28cm). Fold each piece in half, matching up the short sides. (Each page measures 7¾" x 5½" [20cm x 14cml.) Burnish the fold lines well with a bone folder.

Cut out hinges

Copy the template on page 127, enlarge it to 135%, trace it onto a piece of cardstock and cut it out to make a template. Place the saw-tooth edge of the template along the fold line of one of the pages and paperclip it in place. You may mark the triangular cut-outs with a pencil, remove the template and cut them out, or cut directly from the template (as shown).

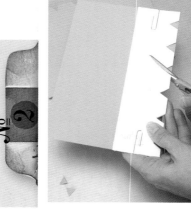

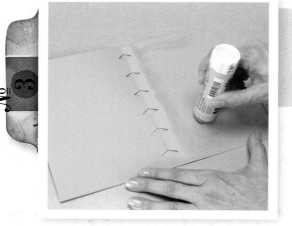

Create book covers

Apply PVA glue to one entire side of the front cover, except for the cut-out areas. Fold the two sides of the page together, creating a double-thick page. Repeat for the back cover.

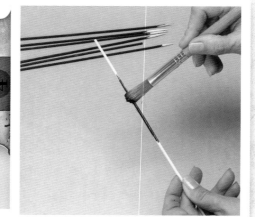

Paint bamboo sticks

Paint seven bamboo sticks black (or the color of your choice) with acrylic paint or gesso. Allow the sticks to dry.

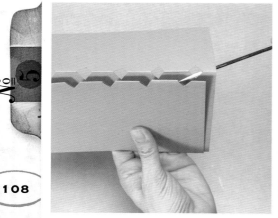

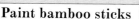

Begin to link pages

Place the front cover on top of one of the folded pages. Insert the pointed end of the stick into the first section at the top of the folded page, then into section two of the cover, section three of the folded page, and so on, until the stick is woven through to the bottom of the page. Allow approximately ¼" (5mm) of the stick to protrude from the top. The pointed bottoms will be trimmed when the book is complete.

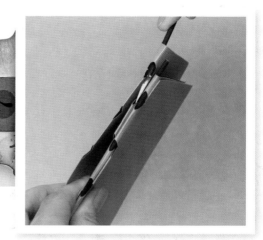

Line up next page

Place another folded page behind the two linked pages, lining up the triangular cut-outs.

Connect next page with bamboo stick

Weave the bamboo stick in and out of alternating sections of each page as in step five.

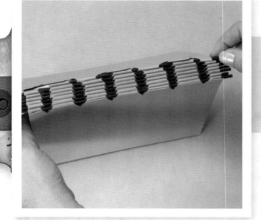

Continue linking pages

Continue lining up pages and weaving bamboo sticks to link them together until all the interior pages and the back cover are connected.

Trim away bottoms of sticks

Make sure all of the sticks are evenly aligned at the top of the page. Use a small pair of garden shears or a strong pair of old scissors (not good paper scissors, please!) to trim off the bottom of the sticks. About ¼" (5mm) of the sticks should protrude from the pages.

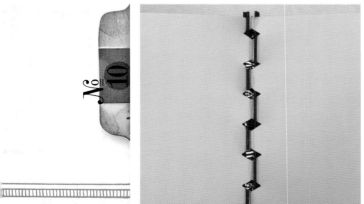

Open book to check construction

When you open your book, you can see how the construction works—just like a piano hinge!

The story behind this layout is simple: These are just a few of the **everyday things I enjoy**, like flowers blooming outside my door, books I collect and girly pleasures like pedicures, beads, makeup and ribbon. I used an artsy alteration technique, Polaroid manipulation, to showcase my favorites on this layout. The result is a photo with the look of an impressionist painting. You can even add some surreal background details like I did in the flip-flops photo.

chronicling tip

TAKE PICTURES OF SEEMINGLY ORDINARY THINGS, LIKE YOUR FAVORITE NAIL POLISH COLOR OR THE FIRST ROSE OF THE SEASON ON THE BUSH IN YOUR YARD. OR, JOURNAL ABOUT THE BOOK YOU READ LAST WEEK. THESE LITTLE DETAILS ARE GLIMPSES INTO YOUR PERSONALITY THAT WON'T SHOW UP IN MOST FAMILY SCRAPBOOKS OR PHOTO ALBUMS. THEY'LL GIVE YOUR CHILDREN AN IDEA OF WHAT YOU WERE LIKE AT THIS POINT IN YOUR LIFE.

SUPPLIES
for the Technique

POLAROID SX-70 LAND CAMERA

POLAROID TIME ZERO FILM

STYLUS, SMALL PAINTBRUSHES OR OTHER ROUNDED TIPS YOU CAN USE TO MANIPULATE PHOTOS

WARM WORK SURFACE *(such as a warm tile)*

COLORED PERMANENT MARKER

RUB-ONS *(paperWERX, Making Memories)*

GLAZE PEN *(Sakura)*

SUPPLIES
to Complete the Project

PATTERNED PAPER *(paperWERX, Creative Imaginations)*

CORRUGATED CARDBOARD

ACRYLIC PAINT *(Delta)*

STAPLES *(Making Memories)*

GLUE STICK

MONOADHESIVE *(TombowUSA)*

family

tip YOU CAN EXPERIMENT WITH MAKING DIFFERENT DESIGNS ON YOUR PHOTO USING ROUNDED-TIP TOOLS. TRY USING A LIGHT CIRCULAR MOTION OR A FEATHERING MOTION TO ADD DIFFERENT TEXTURES TO YOUR IMAGE.

Take photo and allow film to process

Load the Land Camera with film and take a picture. Allow the image to develop fully (colors should be bright). The developing process can take from 5 to 15 minutes.

Manipulate film

Press gently into the photo using a tool with a small tip to create dark lines. Black lines show only in light areas, and white lines show only in dark areas. Be careful not to press too hard, as you'll create unwanted black marks on your image. It is helpful to lay the photo on a warm surface while working to keep the emulsion soft.

Outline photo borders

Outline the photo borders with a colored permanent marker.

Add text to photo

Add text to the photo with rub-on words, and add handwritten words and phrases to the text with a glaze pen, if desired.

construction **notes**

Adhere your manipulated Polaroid photos to a piece of patterned or handpainted paper with a glue stick. Then layer the paper onto a lightly painted piece of corrugated cardboard. I highlighted the title on the bottom of the patterned paper with a glaze pen to give it a raised effect and really make it "pop."

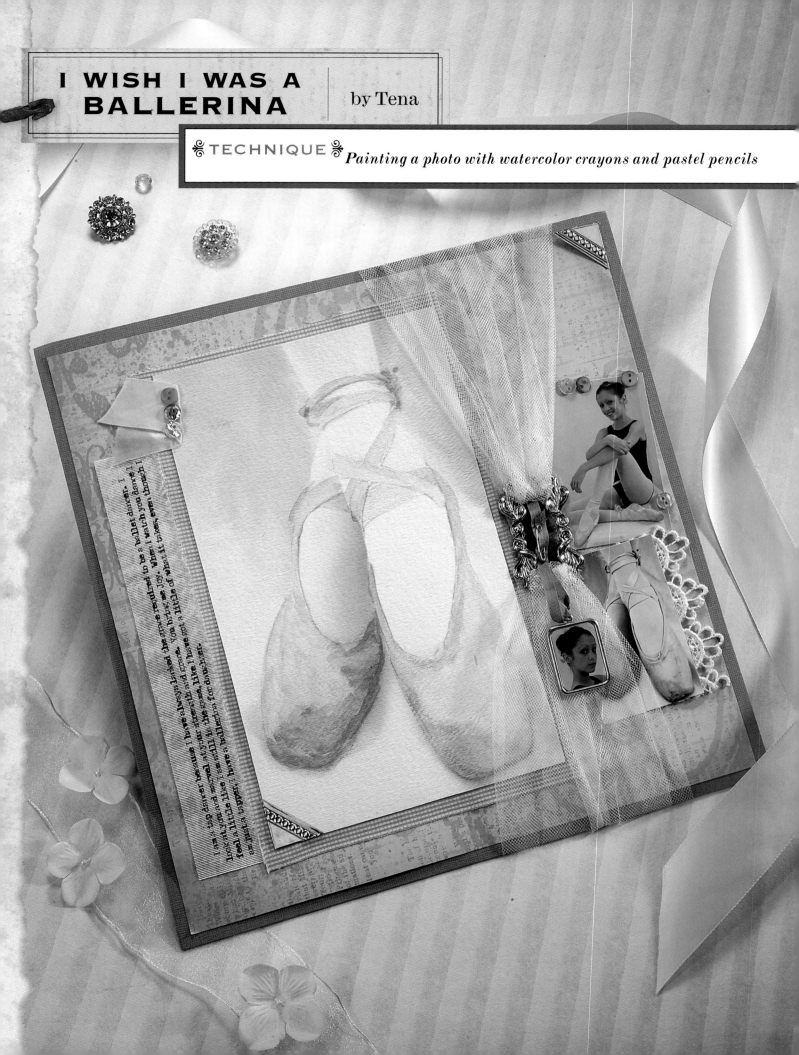

I WISH I WAS A BALLERINA

by Tena

❧ TECHNIQUE ❧ *Painting a photo with watercolor crayons and pastel pencils*

Dance has been a part of my life for as long as I can remember. My mother started me in dance classes when I was just four years old, and it was obvious I had rhythm, but perhaps not grace! My first love in dance was tap, because you can make a lot of noise and get a little crazy, and there's lots of room for freestyle movement. I dabbled in ballet but failed miserably. It thrills me that my daughter excels at all forms of dance, including ballet. This photo of the worn and battered pointe shoes on her feet is **one of my favorites**. I love it when pointe shoes look like they are just starting to feel like a glove on the dancer's feet. The softness of this technique seemed perfect for such elegant subject matter.

chronicling **tip**

THIS TECHNIQUE MAKES US ALL FEEL LIKE REAL ARTISTS! YOU MAY WANT TO EXPERIMENT WITH PASTEL OIL PAINTS THAT ARE SPECIFICALLY DESIGNED TO TINT PHOTOS, OR TRY DIGITAL TOOLS ON YOUR COMPUTER FOR ARTISTICALLY ALTERING IMAGES.

family

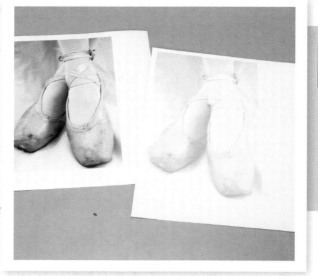

Print washed-out image onto watercolor paper

Insert a digital photo into a Word document, and use the washout feature to lighten the image. (If you'd prefer to use Photoshop, use the desaturate feature.) Print the washed-out image onto 140-pound (300gsm) cold-press watercolor paper. (If necessary, cut the paper down to fit in the printer.)

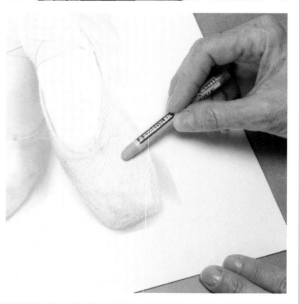

Apply watercolor crayon to image

Using the photo as a guide, apply the watercolor crayon lightly to the surface of the photo.

Go over crayon with water

Moisten a small paintbrush with a bit of water. Use the paintbrush to blend the crayon to resemble paint. Continue adding crayon and brushing over with water until you're happy with the results.

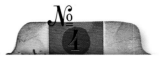

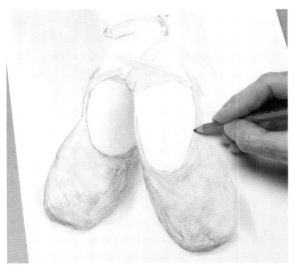

Add definition with pastel pencils

Go over the painted image with pastel pencils to add definition where needed.

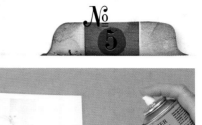

Spray image with fixative

When the image is filled in as you like it, spray it with a fixative to prevent fading or smearing.

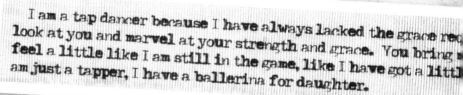

I am a tap dancer because I have always lacked the grace re
look at you and marvel at your strength and grace. You bring
feel a little like I am still in the game, like I have got a littl
am just a tapper, I have a ballerina for daughter.

discover **me**

JESSIE BALDWIN

My scrapbooks are full—full of pages about my children, my husband, my family and my childhood. But I have very few pages about me as I am now. I want my children to be able to read about me and my life at thirty years old. I want them to see a photo of me as myself—with a few pounds to lose, being a little silly. I want them to remember me like this. I want them to discover me as more than a mom: as a person.

celebrate · sparkle · shine · love · give

understand · adore · listen · hope · dream

I AM: 30 years old
I WANT: chocolate ;)
I HAVE: two children and a husband
I WISH: I took more everyday photos before I had kids
I HATE: to fold laundry
I MISS: my sisters
I HEAR: my kids singing silly songs in the backseat of my car
I WONDER: if I will grow old gracefully
I AM NOT: as organized as people think
I ALWAYS: stop at a kid's lemonade stand
I SING: when no one can hear me
I LAUGH: when I see my son's naked butt
I CRY: every time I watch "Return to Me"
I MAKE WITH MY HANDS: works of art
I WRITE: in journals whenever I travel
I REGRET: not playing Scrabble before my 29th birthday
I NEED: to exercise more
I SHOULD: eat healthier too

101 things to do **before i die**

LAURIE STAMAS

I was shopping one day when a book with this title caught my eye, and I decided I should create a list of my own. I created bookmark-type tags listing my "101 Things to Do" so I can check them off as they are accomplished. Then, I created my own background paper by typing all of the items on the list so they would be more visible and reinforce the theme.

This hardback book shell/mini clipboard journal offers a synergy of ways to incorporate photos, journaling and memorabilia in a cutting-edge, altered concept. I think it is important to create "self-journals." Whether it's through a photo shoot or journaling to express your thoughts, dreams, accomplishments, hardships and inspirations, I believe in putting it all out there—nothing to hide. This is me, visually and through my words.

you make **me fly**
CÉLINE NAVARRO

I wanted to do a tribute to love with this piece. The woman in the picture is one of my ancestors, but nobody can tell me who she is. I think she looks sad and lost, and I wanted to create a different story for her. Here's the story: She is, in fact, madly in love with a soldier gone to war, and she is impatiently waiting for him to come back. Their love is like no other—bright, strong and true. Just like my color palette!

in my 30s
and loving it
KATHERINE BROOKS

I have come to terms with the fact that I am in my thirties, and life is good! I was inspired to create an album about the things I enjoy, the love I feel and the dreams I have in my thirties. I teach scrapbook classes and am always amazed at how many women do not create projects about themselves. I want to leave behind a sense of who I am, and I hope this artwork will be something my children will cherish and share with their families.

what's inside
HEIDI SWAPP

Right now, it seems like being pregnant is all I can think about. I had my husband snap a few photos of my rounded state for this layout. I wanted to show my excitement for the baby to be here. I know I still have so much left to do before baby can come, but I can't help wondering what I am having, what he or she will look like and how it will feel to have a new one in my arms again.

OH HOW I LOVE THAT SWEET ISLAND BEAT

Prayer for the world · Its a long long way · Red Red wine · Bring me your cup · Wild wild Life · Hurry come up · Many rivers to cross · She caught the train · Temptress · Underneath it all · Human work it out · Just a little bit longer · C'est La Vie · Cherry oh Baby · Version · Surefire · Cool me down · Temperature · Shut up · Tell it like it is ·

When I think of music that is happy and soothing... It's always reggae for me. The island beat is in my car, on my ipod and in my music collection. Yea Mon!

Bob Marley · UB40 · Sean Paul · Maxi Priest · The Wailing Souls · Azz Izz · Jimmy Cliff

island **beat**
TENA SPRENGER

I can't remember the first time I heard reggae music, but it seems like I have always loved it. Reggae soothes my soul. When I hear it, I relax and slip into the rhythm. It's great to dance to, to create art to, to sip a margarita on the beach to—it even makes housework more pleasant! My husband loves it too, and some of our earliest dates were to go listen to local reggae bands and dance. That's just one more reason I love that sweet island beat!

sometimes you just gotta **play!**
CAROL WINGERT

After experiencing a brief creative block, I started playing with some stretched canvases and new paints. I arranged fabrics, buttons and vintage flowers in a box and took photos, which I printed and added to the canvas. From this, an idea was born to create a folio from two hinged canvases. Inside the little framed spaces, I included mini glass jars of paint, a sawed-off paintbrush and little cardstock tubes covered with some of the fabrics I photographed. I didn't just rediscover my creativity: I had a colorful, unique project to show it off!

AWAKEN YOUR CREATIVITY: PLAY

Resources

All of the materials used in the projects in this book can be purchased at your local craft, fabric, hardware, home improvement, scrapbooking, rubber-stamping or discount department stores. If you are unable to find what you need at a local store, contact the manufacturers listed below for a retailer near you.

7gypsies
www.7gypsies.com
paper, embellishments

AccuCut
www.accucut.com
die cuts

AMACO, Inc.
www.amaco.com
paint, finishes, clay, tools

American Crafts, Inc.
www.americancrafts.com
ribbon

American Crafts
www.americancrafts.com
ribbon

Ampersand Art Supply
www.ampersandart.com
scratchboard, tools

Autumn Leaves
www.autumnleaves.com
paper, embellishments

Avery Dennison Corporation
www.avery.com
office supplies, adhesives, school supplies, ink

BasicGrey, LLC
www.basicgrey.com
paper, embellishments

Bazzill Basics Paper Inc.
www.bazzillbasics.com
cardstock, embellishments

Bo-Bunny Press
www.bobunny.com
paper, embellishments

Canvas Concepts
www.canvasconcepts.com
canvas home decor

Captured Elements, LLC
www.capturedelements.com
patterned paper

Cavallini, Papers & Co., Inc.
www.cavallini.com
stationery, paper, gifts

Creative Imaginations
www.cigift.com
embellishments

Cretacolor
www.cretacolor.com
colored pencils

Daylab
www.daylab.com
Daylab equipment, accessories

DCC
www.dcccrafts.com
papier mâché boxes, torsos

Delish Designs
www.delishdesigns.com
paper, rub-ons, chipboard, embellishments

Delta Technical Coatings Inc.
www.deltacrafts.com
craft paint

Deluxe Designs
www.deluxecuts.com
die cuts, embellishments

DMD Industries, Inc.
www.dmdind.com
paper

Doodlebug Designs
www.doodlebug.ws
paper, embellishments

Duncan Enterprises
www.duncancrafts.com
tacky glue

EK Success
www.eksuccess.com
paper, embellishments

Eclectic Products, Inc.
www.eclecticproducts.com
E-6000 glue

Fancy Pants Designs, LLC
www.fancypantsdesigns.com
patterned paper

Fiskars Brands, Inc.
www.fiskars.com
eyelet lace punch, scissors

Flair Designs
www.flairdesignsinc.com
embellishments, charms

FolkArt
www.plaidonline.com
paint

FontWerks
www.fontwerks.com
rubber stamps, paper

Fredrix
www.fredrixartistcanvas.com
artist canvas

Golden Artist Colors, Inc.
www.goldenpaints.com
gel mediums, gesso, tar gel

Grafix
www.grafixarts.com
self-adhesive transparencies

Green Pepper Press
www.greenpepperpress.com
rubber stamps

Heidi Swapp
www.heidiswapp.com
embellishments, chipboard products, foam stamps, masks

Hero Arts
www.heroarts.com
rubber stamps

Iota
www.everyiota.com
paper

Jacquard Products
www.jacquardproducts.com
printable fabric

JudiKins, Inc.
www.judikins.com
Diamond Glaze, rubber stamps

Junkitz
www.junkitz.com
embellishments

K&Company, Inc.
www.kandcompany.com
paper, embellishments

KI Memories, Inc.
www.kimemories.com
scrapbook paper

Karen Foster Design, Inc.
www.karenfosterdesign.com
embellishments

Krylon Products Group
www.krylon.com
paint, glazes, finishes

Limited Edition Rubberstamps
www.limitededitionrs.com
rubber stamps

Lineco, Inc.
www.lineco.com
PVA glue, book board

Liquitex Artist Materials
www.liquitex.com
paint products, artist mediums

Magic Scraps–Advantus Corp.
www.magicscraps.com
paper, embellishments, adhesives

Magistical Memories
www.magisticalmemories.com
chipboard alphabets

Making Memories
www.makingmemories.com
paper, foam stamps, paint, embellishments

Matisse Derivan
www.matisse.com.au
paints, gesso

MercArt USA, LLC
www.mercartusa.com
crafters metal, metal working tools

Michael Miller Memories, LLC
www.michaelmillermemories.com
fabric paper, fabric

My Mind's Eye
www.mymindseye.com
paper, embellishments, rub-ons

Mysticpress.com
embellishments

paperWERX
www.lazarstudiowerx.com
patterned paper, image transfers

Pixie Press LLC
www.pixiepress.com
indexed book board

Plaid Enterprises, Inc.
www.plaidonline.com
craft paint, Mod Podge

Polaroid Corporation
www.polaroid.com
film, SX-70 Land Camera

Postmodern Design Rubber Stamps
(405) 321-3176
rubber stamps

Pressed Petals
www.pressedpetals.com
paper, chipboard, embellishments

Primamarketing Inc.
www.primamarketinginc.com
paper flowers

Provo Craft and Novelty
www.provocraft.com
embellishments

Prym Consumer USA Inc.
www.dritz.com
large grommets

QuicKutz, Inc.
www.quickutz.com
die-cutting tools, die cuts

Rag & Bone Bindery Ltd.
www.ragandbonebindery.com
handmade journals

Ranger Industries Inc.
www.rangerink.com
ink

Renaissance Art LLC
(860) 567-2785
mini wooden windows

Rusty Pickle
www.rustypickle.com
paper, embellishments

Sakura Color Products of America
www.gellyroll.com
pens, art mediums

Saunders Mfg. Co. Inc.
www.saunders-usa.com
UHU glue stick

Scenic Route Paper Co.
www.scenicroutepaper.com
paper, embellishments

SEI
www.shopsei.com
scrapbook paper, embellishments

STAEDTLER USA
www.staedtler-usa.com
watercolor crayons, pencils

Stampendous, Inc.
www.stampendous.com
rubber stamps

Stampers Anonymous
www.stampersanonymous.com
rubber stamps

Stampington & Co.
www.stampington.com
rubber stamps

Stampotique Originals, Inc.
www.stampotique.com
rubber stamps

Stewart Gill
www.stewartgill.com
paints, fresco flakes

Strathmore Artist Papers
www.mohawkpaper.com
watercolor paper

Sunday International
www.sundayint.com
rubber stamps

Three Bugs in a Rug, LLC
www.3bugsinarug.com
paper

TombowUSA
www.tombowusa.com
adhesive products

Tsukineko, Inc.
www.tsukineko.com
ink

Umbra, Ltd.
www.umbra.com
photo albums

ABOUT THE
guest artists

heidi swapp is living the scrapbooker's dream! What started out as a passion for scrapbooking, photography and pretty paper has turned into a full-blown career for this thirty-four-year-old mother of four. Armed with seven years of teaching on local, national and international levels, the experience of conceiving and producing multiple idea books, and a couple of years designing products for Making Memories, Heidi ventured out to create her own line of products. Now, through Advantus Corp., she develops innovative and fresh products for the scrapbooking industry. Heidi continues to be the vision and creative force behind her brand, as well as directing its marketing and education efforts. Despite the challenge of it all, she has not lost her love of artistic creation and exploration. She still lives for a day that she will stay in pajamas all day long, free to lose track of time in her studio.

From the time she was a child, **jessie** baldwin wanted to be an artist, but it wasn't until she discovered scrapbooking that she realized the true artist within her. She considers each page her "canvas" and proudly displays much of her art on the walls of her house rather than in albums. She has been recognized for her work in several major industry contests: as a finalist in the 2004 Make It Meaningful Contest, as one of ten winners in the international 2005 Memory Makers Masters Competition, and as Honorable Mention in the 2005 *Creating Keepsakes* Hall of Fame. Jessie has been published in all of the leading scrapbook industry magazines and has contributed to several books. Jessie graduated from UNLV in 1997 with a degree in elementary education and taught for several years. Most recently, she worked part-time as the art director for a local private school. She has now retired from teaching to focus solely on making her art and raising her kids, both of which challenge her creatively! She lives in Las Vegas with her husband, Rick, and her two children, Violet and Riley.

kelly anderson has been published in various publications, including *Creating Keepsakes*, *PaperART*, *Simple Scrapbooks* and *Better Homes and Gardens*. Her work is featured in the books *Artful Memories*, *Full Circle*, *Hot Looks for Scrapbooks*, *7gypsies in Paris*, *Creating Keepsakes Elements* and *Creating Keepsakes Artistic Effects*. She is also in the 2002 *Creating Keepsakes* Hall of Fame. Kelly lives in Tempe, Arizona, with her husband, Tony, and daughter, Madelyn.

céline navarro is a twenty-five-year-old self-taught artist living in Montpellier, Southern France. Collaborative projects are among her favorite things in the art world. She has always loved to trade with other people, to be involved in round robins and share ideas, techniques and tips. She's currently involved in several projects with big names and is working on her own books in France. She's been published in several magazines, including *The ATC Book* by Stampington, *Somerset Home*, *The Stamper's Sampler*, *Scrapbook Answers*, *Legacy* and *Somerset Studio*. She teaches in France, throughout Europe and in the United States.

laurie stamas, a freelance designer and instructor, began scrapbooking about eight years ago. Her work has been published by *Creating Keepsakes*, *Better Homes and Gardens* and Pinecone Press. She has also done design work for Artistic Expressions, Autumn Leaves, Lasting Impressions, Scrapbook.com, SEI and others. Laurie is a 2004 *Creating Keepsakes* Hall of Fame winner and has enjoyed teaching classes at *Creating Keepsakes* conventions for the last couple of years. Laurie lives in Arizona with her husband, Jim, and their two teenage daughters, Alexia and Stephanie.

katherine brooks is a full-time designer and senior educator for Deluxe Designs who has authored more than four idea books for the company. She is a 2004 *Creating Keepsakes* Hall of Fame winner and has been published in numerous magazines and idea books. Katherine enjoys creating scrapbook pages, altered art and jewelry in her free time. When not traveling all over the United States teaching, Katherine can be found at home with her husband of twelve years, John, and her two children, Meghan (age ten) and Matt (age six).

stephanie mcAtee has always had passion for the elements of art, especially collage, photography and journaling. She discovered scrapbooking five years ago, and in the time since, she feels like she has finally evolved and found her style. Stephanie has been a part of numerous design teams, has designed her own product lines and in April 2005 started her own company, Captured Elements. Her passion to express herself through her art is driven by her family: Rich, Bobby and Ethan. They inspire her; they appreciate her art; they are her life elements, no matter what. Stephanie resides in Kansas City, Missouri.

Index

Enlarge template to 135% for use with It's Good to Be Queen, pages 106–109.

Find Artful Inspiration in these other North Light Titles!

Artful Memories
by Carol Wingert and Tena Sprenger

Inside *Artful Memories*, co-authors Carol Wingert and Tena Sprenger show you how to take your memory art to the next level by creatively combining traditional artist's mediums with fabric, papercrafting and bookmaking supplies. From image transfers to book binding, *Artful Memories* combines the hottest techniques in the memory art world to help crafters make the most of their treasured memories. Choose from more than 30 step-by-step projects and get inspired by the fabulous gallery sections for each chapter.

ISBN-10: 1-58180-810-0, ISBN-13: 978-1-58180-810-0, paperback, 128 pages, #33488

Collage Lost and Found
by Josie Cirincione

Inside *Collage Lost and Found*, you'll learn how to find and use old photographs, memorabilia and ephemera to create collages based on your heritage. Using her own Sicilian background as an example, author Josie Cirincione shows you how to examine your own heritage for inspiration, as well as tips on where to look and what to look for. Then you'll choose from 20 step-by-step projects that use basic collage, jewelry-making and image transfer techniques to make sassy projects to decorate with, wear and give away as gifts.

ISBN-10: 1-58180-787-2, ISBN-13: 978-1-58180-787-5, paperback, 128 pages, #33461

Expressions
by Donna Smylie and Allison Tyler Jones

Compelling, memorable photographs are the centerpiece of any scrapbook. Now, scrapbooking and memory art enthusiasts have a photography instruction book written just for them. *Expressions* reveals how to create extraordinary photos that will make any scrapbook or display project a vivid record of special events and everyday life. Focusing on portraiture, the book follows the family life cycle, from babies to grandparents, with each subject explored from a fresh perspective.

ISBN 10: 1-58180-909-3, ISBN-13: 978-1-58180-909-1, paperback, 128 pages, #Z0526

These and other fine North Light titles are available from your local art and craft retailers, bookstores or online suppliers.